An **Inside** Job

An Inside Job

A SPIRITUAL APPROACH TO
FINDING YOUR RIGHT WORK

G. Richard Rieger

UNITY® Books
Unity Village, Missouri

First Edition 1999

To receive a catalog of all our Unity publications (books, cassettes, compact discs, and magazines) or to place an order, call our Customer Service Department: (816) 969-2069 or 1-800-669-0282.

The publisher wishes to acknowledge the editorial work of Michael Maday, Raymond Teague, and Joanne Englehart; the copyediting of Thomas Lewin; the production help of Rozanne Devine and Jane Blackwood; and the marketing efforts of Allen Liles and Sharon Sartin.

Cover design by Diane Marshall

The New Revised Standard Version is used for all Bible verses, unless otherwise stated.

Library of Congress Cataloging-in-Publication Data

Rieger, Richard, 1928–
    An inside job x: a spiritual approach to finding your right work / G. Richard Rieger. —1st ed.
      p.   cm.
    Includes bibliographical references (p.).
    ISBN 0-87159-227-4 (pbk.)
    1. Vocation—Christianity. 2. Unity School of Christianity—Doctrines. I. Title.
BX9890.U505R54   1999
248.8'8—dc21   98-41062
                                       CIP

Dedication

I dedicate this book
to my best friend, co-worker,
and beloved wife, Marilyn,
who led me into my right work
and continues to
believe in me.

Acknowledgments

For each of us, if we will listen, there is a continuous stream of creative ideas passing through our mind—flowing from the Source of all ideas. Some call it "the voice of intuition"; others, "the still small voice." Poets and musicians call it their "creative Muse." To this Source I am eternally thankful.

My deepest love and gratitude to my mother, who raised me with spiritual principles and placed my feet upon the spiritual pathway; to Charles and Myrtle Fillmore, who laid a firm foundation; and to Emma Curtis Hopkins, Emmet Fox, and other spiritual teachers who have opened me to the higher understanding of my true nature. I am grateful also to the "strangers" I have met on the pathway of life who—in a passing remark or action—gave me just the right insight I needed at that moment.

Invaluable guidance came from conversations with my very close and special friend Auriel, without whom this book could not have been written.

I am also grateful to the people in my workshops who shared many ideas with me in our discussions together. I want to thank my friend of many years, Alan

Kamman, whose fine insights on "Menta-Miracles" I have quoted, and who has worked many of the ideas presented here in his own successful business career. I also am thankful for the inspiration of Mother Meera. My appreciation goes out to other dear and supportive friends, among them Joyce Browne, Linda Koe, Barbara Dalberg, and Pat Richter, for their encouragement and review of the manuscript.

My thanks again to Marilyn for her valuable insights into ways to improve the book and for patiently proofreading the revisions. God bless her!

Table of Contents

Preparing Yourself for Your Right Work

Chapter 1

Working With Your Inner Employment Counselor

If you are looking for your right work, you need to be looking in the right place—and that right place is within you. Let me explain.

Work in the twenty-first century is not something we do; it is something done through us. It is an inside job. We no longer work on our own, but in partnership with the Creative Intelligence within us. It supplies the ideas, and our part is to do the leg work.

So to find your right work you must first contact your Inner Employment Counselor and agree to listen and follow through on Its guidance. This Inner Partner will not only lead you to the work It desires to accomplish through you, but It will accomplish that work through you as well. No longer will you be working by the "sweat of your brow"—your own limited intellect—but instead you will be tuning in to the Higher Wisdom of your Inner Partner.

So your most important job right now is to make the all-important choice to join in that creative partnership.

As you make that commitment, the universe immediately moves to help you.

Goethe wrote:

> The moment one definitely commits oneself then Providence moves too; all sorts of things occur to help one that would never otherwise have occurred. A whole stream of events issues from the decision of unforeseen incidents and meetings and material assistance which no man could have dreamt would come his way.[1]

If you have ever experienced one of those rare days when everything flows in perfect order—when all the traffic lights are green, the things you need are right there when you need them, and the people you need to meet come into your life at exactly the right time—that is a small sample of what happens when you make the commitment to work with your Inner Partner.

This inner commitment puts you into a flow of synchronous ideas and events. "Chance" remarks, "coincidences," or apparent "detours" become the clues to the right work that your Inner Partner wants

WORKING WITH YOUR INNER EMPLOYMENT COUNSELOR · 3

to show you. You have only to cultivate that connection, stay open, and "go with the flow of Spirit."

Your Inner Partner is continually prompting you to follow certain leads, and if you will learn to listen to and act upon these promptings—in spite of the arguments of your logic—you will be rewarded with success. Work to develop a moment-by-moment, conscious listening habit.

The first step, then, in preparing yourself for your right work is learning to listen to and trust your Inner Guidance and courageously act upon it. Trusting in this Inner Guidance is the way of the twenty-first century. Just as the previous centuries of the Industrial Age were dominated by the intellect, cold logic, and ruthlessness, so the new century will give credence to the power of the intuitive side of our nature and honor the higher instincts in man. Already this shift is occurring.

Dee Hock, business genius and innovative creator of the global Visa credit card network, intuited this transformational shift and sees the vast changes that are coming in the new millennium:

> We are at that very point in time when a 400-year-old age is dying and another is struggling to be born—a shifting of culture, science, society, and institutions enormously greater than the world has ever experienced. Ahead, the possibility of the regeneration of individuality, liberty, community, and ethics such as the world has never known, and a harmony with nature, with

4 · An Inside Job

one another, and with the divine intelligence such as the world has never dreamed.[2]

This is the vision with which we align ourselves when we shift to working intuitively with our Inner Partner—the Divine Intelligence within us.

We did not come here to plod through life working for the "Almighty Dollar." We came to work for the Almighty—that is, to fulfill a role that each of us was pre-equipped to play in the Creator's Mutual Support System.

If we view life from the highest perspective, we see that our true purpose is to nourish the world through which we flow. When we do, our life is "green" and fruitful. It takes on its true meaning and we prosper like riverbanks that are always green—nourished by the living waters they channel.

Matthew Fox wrote: "A dried-up person and dried-up culture lose their ability to create. . . . Our work is meant to be a green work, a greening work, a creative work."[3]

If at present you are feeling frustrated and unhappy with your life and work, it is because you are feeling there is something more to life: something beyond what the world considers to be the reasons for working—to put food in our belly, pay the mortgage, care for the family, and enjoy as many toys and pleasures as we can before exiting.

Those reasons are not enough. They do not satisfy that gnawing hunger for fulfillment. It can't be assuaged by a new toy or a new adventure, a new romance, or anything else the world has to offer.

Perhaps you have recently left your job or lost it, or perhaps you are just starting out in the work world— feeling your way along, wondering what it is you are supposed to do with your life. Perhaps you are at the halfway mark and are hitting the stone wall of midlife disappointment. You have not achieved the success you saw shining ahead of you when you were back at the beginning of the ladder. You feel you still have not expressed what is inside you, and worse yet, you are not even sure what that is. You simply have the vague feeling that there has to be something more.

You are like the old-time gold prospector digging a ton of ore to get a little bit of gold. That is what all of those outer things offer—a little bit of pleasure or reward, just enough to keep us digging away, but not enough to satisfy.

The truth is that your life's journey, complete with its detours, has been leading you to the place where you can express the God-given talents you were born to share with the world.

All of your experiences and all of the people who have ever touched your life have in some way been preparing you for your right expression. When you find it, you will be fulfilling what you came into this world to do. You will be working from your passion instead of the spreadsheet.

All of our inner discomfort in life stems from withholding or impounding our innate creativity and love. If we do not express what we came to express, create what we came to create, and share the love we are, then that creativity and love, in its struggle to be born, creates internal havoc in our minds and bodies and external havoc in our affairs.

If you are experiencing restlessness, illness, or difficulty in your life right now, it is a sign your creativity is being thwarted and is pushing to come forth.

Viktor Frankl wrote: "Everyone has his own specific vocation or mission in life; everyone must carry out a concrete assignment that demands fulfillment. Therein he cannot be replaced, nor can his life be repeated. Thus, everyone's task is as unique as is his specific opportunity to implement it."[4]

The Truth is that you are part of a larger plan and that you have been endowed with a unique combination of talents and abilities through which your Inner Partner desires to be expressed. Open yourself, step aside, and say to your Partner: "Work through me; create through me. Place me where You can make the best use of the talents You have given to me."

As you do so, you will be synchronizing yourself with the great Universal Mutual Support System in which everything is mutually supportive of everything else, in perfect rhythm and harmony. Our assignment is part of this larger plan, and we have a unique role to play. Your place in this universal order is outlined in the following statement. As you read it aloud to yourself, let it reinforce your sense of being part of this larger purpose.

Inner Activity #1   Statement of Purpose

There is Something within me that knows the way
to my right expression.
It is the Infinite Intelligence which created me—
the All-knowing Mind which knows how and where
and when. As I consciously align myself with It,
I am shown the way to my good.
My Self-empowerment lies in my staying tuned
to this Source—
for from It flows all that I
ever need to succeed in life.
I was created to function as part
of a Universal Mutual Support System.
For every demand, Infinite Intelligence has also
created the right supply. I am part of that supply,
as well as part of the demand.
There is no need for me to feel discouraged.
The truth is that I have been endowed with a unique
combination of talents, resources, and energies
which the world needs.
No one else has these in quite the same
combination as I do.
Thus, I am automatically guaranteed a role to play,
for I am an essential part of the Whole.

Your Inner Wisdom knows the way to that role. It
knows how and where and when. Many years ago, I
visited a woman lying in a hospital bed. She shared a
powerful statement with me that speaks to this Truth.

Her name was Myrtle Dark, and she had spent her life inspiring and empowering others. At the time, we were talking about possible new directions for her life—a "What next, Lord?" conversation.

She smiled confidently and said:

"The Mind that knows how—is showing me now,
The Mind that knows where—is leading me there.
The Mind that knows when—will tell me then."

The peace and the sheer strength of that assurance struck me deeply. I have used it over the years whenever I was feeling that I had lost my way. Tune in to this "Mind that knows," and It will lead you "there"—to the right expression of your talents.

Its promptings are those small whispers in the back of your mind. They are fleeting and difficult to hear amid the noisy chatter of the ego mind, but you can access them by pausing to take a deep breath and silently asking "What next, Lord?" for a few quiet moments. You may want to take a few deep, quiet breaths and do this right now. Slow down and listen.

People ask, "How can I know which voice is the right one?" The answer is, "You will know it by the feelings of light and peace that it gives you." There is no heaviness or darkness associated with ideas received from the "still small voice" of your Inner Partner. Follow that peace in the midst of the ego mind's static, and it will bring you safely to your destination, as the invisible radio navigation beam guides an airline pilot safely through the overcast.

If you stop and think about it, the main stumbling block to finding your right work is the continual worrying of your fearful intellect. It worries because it is incapable of leading you to a place where it has never been before. But the intuitive side of your nature—in constant contact with the Creative Mind within you—knows the way through the uncharted territory to your right place. It will take you safely there.

One man who learned to listen intuitively is Ted Hoff of the Intel Corporation. He was the main inventor of the microchip, which revolutionized the computer industry and made possible the downsizing of huge, room-sized mainframes to small personal computers. The tiny chips are the brains of everything from the global Internet to our kitchen microwaves. They are the logos of the twenty-first century.

If Hoff had not invented the chip, someone else would have, because the idea "was in the air."

Ideas are universal—available to anyone who will listen and follow through on them. They wait like water behind a tap, ready to flow. Opening our minds to the flow means a daily time of listening. For some this means a quiet time of meditation; for others it may mean a morning walk that gets the ideas flowing. A daydream led Albert Einstein to the theory of relativity. A teenage student in Zurich, he had a vision of riding along a light beam. With his prepared mind, Einstein realized he had traveled in a curved line, which gave him his revolutionary insight that changed the entire field of physics.

Robert Boger, a multimillionaire textile manufac-
turer, asked for ideas from the Source while in his
morning shower, and he wouldn't come out until he
received one—to the great vexation of his frugal Ger-
man wife!

Boger was a friend of my parents when I was a
child. He had emigrated from Germany as a youth
and had become a "self-made man." If he heard me
use that term, he would probably say "a Self-made
man," because he was in touch with his Higher Self,
the Source of his success. I remember him riding up to
our house in his chauffeur-driven car and staying long
hours to discuss with my mother the role that spiritual intuition played in his success. In rough hand-
written notes, she had recorded fragments of those
conversations:

A concentration on a definite goal without
any conscious desire for material gain . . . giving freely with open mind, not extravagantly
but thoughtfully, knowing the rule of nature
that you cannot receive without giving . . . does
not immediately manifest itself. Incidentally,
[his intuition] is always active on Friday. Large
business events have transpired on a Friday, but
[Robert] does not make conscious use of it.

"[Robert] desired a specific knowledge, con-
sistently concentrated on one thought—was
rewarded with a key idea forcefully delivered,
like seeing a sudden light equal to a halo—a re-
markable experience, still very vivid.

Boger knew that his success depended on listening to and working with his Inner Partner. When we work in this intuitive way, we gain a sense of fulfillment that we never feel when we are working by the "sweat of our brow."

The second step in finding your right work is to get into the energy flow of Divine Love, which synchronizes our movements with the overall plan that the Holy Spirit is endeavoring to work through us. Just as electrical energy flows strongest through a line in which there is little or no resistance, so do we work most easily, joyously, and freely when we let Divine Love and harmony flow through us unimpeded— when the resistance of our fears and resentments is removed from the line.

The twenty-first century will be a time in which this power of Love will be increasingly evident on every level of living. It is even now becoming recognized in the corporate world. Margaret Wheatley, a nationally known management consultant, writes of this new philosophy in her insightful book *Leadership and the New Science*:

> Because power is energy, it needs to flow through organizations; it cannot be confined to functions or levels. We have seen the positive results of this flowing organizational energy in our experiences with participative management and self-managed teams. What gives power its charge, positive or negative, is the quality of relationships. Those who relate

through coercion, or from a disregard for the other person, create negative energy. Those who are open to others and who see others in their fullness create positive energy. Love in organizations, then, is the most potent source of power we have available.[5]

In your search for a new work expression, look for those companies operating on these new intuitive and harmonizing principles. They are on the leading edge of consciousness. If you feel led to start your own company, base it on these new principles and work in the energy flow of Divine Love.

Chapter 2

Clearing Away the Hidden Blocks to Your Success

The next step in moving into your right work is to remove the resistance on the line connecting you to your Inner Partner. Just as the flow of electrical current through a wire is restricted by three major factors—the length of the line, heat, and the diameter of the wire—just so the flow of divine ideas, strength, and love from your Source is impeded by your sense of separation, or distance, from God; your emotional heat (anger, fear, and resentment); and the diameter of your faith.

Each of us is like those dimmer switches we have in our homes. The lights are brightest when the electricity is flowing freely, and they dim as we turn the switch, which adds resistance to the line, restricting the flow. If you put your hand on the dimmer switch after it has been on for a while, you will feel heat in the switch.

Our potential to prosper and fully express our God-given talents is bright, but we dim our prospects when we feel alone, unworthy, or separated from the Source of our good. We also restrict the flow of our potential when we feel "hot under the collar" with anger or resentment or when our prayer line to God is too small.

It is impossible to succeed in your right work until you first get right within yourself, and that means clearing your consciousness of the negative mental and emotional resistance blocking the way to your success.

You probably know individuals who change jobs frequently. Many may even be in the higher echelon of the executive ranks. But after a few years in the new position, they encounter the same difficulties that they found in their previous work. What is happening is that they are coming up against the same hidden blocks which sabotaged them in their previous positions. Their self-defeating beliefs and attitudes are blocking the flow of their potential.

Have you ever hiked through the woods and come across a tiny spring seeping forth from under a pile of dead leaves and debris? If you kneel down and scoop away the debris, the spring gushes forth with great energy.

That's the way it is with us. If we are willing to kneel down and clear away all of the trash—our old fears and counterproductive attitudes—the springs of our potential will gush forth with new energy and success. Our lives will be renewed and refreshed.

"Kneeling down" means being willing to surrender our self-centered will, our fears, and our self-limiting beliefs.

Work now to identify that inner debris so you can clear it out and set your inner house of consciousness in order.

Here are four major blocks that sabotage our success: (1) lack of self-worth and a poor self-image, (2) resentments and unforgivenesses, (3) attachment to old work roles and identities, and (4) fear of change and its possible consequences.

FIRST BLOCK:
Overcoming Lack of Self-Worth and a Poor Self-Image

Look over the following list and check any that strike a chord in you as being particularly valid in your thinking right now. They hold clues to the hidden beliefs and attitudes that need to be dissolved so your Inner Partner can work through you.

- Feelings of self-doubt—of not being good enough to compete or step out on your own.
- Fear of being "too old to hire" or of making a new start.

- Fear of your poor past track record repeating itself.
- Fear of leaving the security of an old rut of a job in order to step out on faith to follow your inner guidance.
- Use of loyalty to a job or to people as an excuse for not having the courage to leave.
- Fear of peer pressure or of what others may say such as, "You're going to give up your job to do *what*?"
- Effort to follow a career that is not "you." Trying to fill someone else's expectations of what you should be and do.

Each of these fears stems from not knowing who and what we really are. As long as we believe we are only what we see in the mirror, we can never feel truly confident. Looking into the mirror isn't exactly the best way to convince ourselves that things are improving!

How do you see yourself? More importantly, which self are you seeing? Are you seeing the limited one which appears in the mirror, the one which society and circumstances reflect back to you? This is not your true Self, which is a branch of the "True Vine"— the individual expression of the One—infinitely capable, loved, and worthy.

If you will look deeply into those eyes looking back at you in the mirror, you may catch a glimpse of Someone so powerful that you will catch your breath in awe. Angela Morgan describes this Someone in her poem "Know Thyself":

> It is your own Self driving you,
> Your Self that you have never known,
> Seeing your little self alone.
> Your Self, high-seated charioteer,
> Master of cowardice and fear,
> Your Self that sees the shining length
> Of all the fearful road ahead,
> Knows that the terrors that you dread
> Are pigmies to your splendid strength . . . .
> Your Self that holds the mastering rein,
> Seeing beyond the sweat and pain
> And anguish of your driven soul,
> The patient beauty of the goal![1]

Deep within your soul lives this true Self that is part of something greater than you can ever imagine.

You may feel that you are all alone, struggling to make it through life on your own puny strength. But the truth is that a Power greater than any challenge has sent you into this world to be an instrument through which It can express Its good purposes. As such you are designed for success and vital to the overall plan.

Let the following statement remind you that you are unique and worthy. Photocopy it and tape it on your bathroom mirror, where you can read it aloud to yourself as you start your day.

Inner Activity #2 The Truth About Myself

Regardless of my present self-image or
   opinion of myself or what others may
   think of me,
the real Truth about myself is that deep
   down inside me,
beneath the outer shell of my personality,
beyond any childhood scars and traumas,
beyond any lack of education or past
   failures
or the limitations of my present
   circumstances—
Beyond all of that outer, is my real Self, the
   unique being which my Creator created
   me to be—strong, capable, loving, and
   wise.
I am a unique and valuable individual. I am
   capable and worth loving.
I am an eternal being, now in the process of
   awakening to my true potential.
The process may at times seem tedious or
   even hopeless. It may seem too much to
   bear, too discouraging; but this much I
   know truly
that while I may fail if I try to "go it
   alone"—
The power and intelligence of my Creator's
   presence
in the heart of me cannot fail.

I will succeed, as I let my Higher Power
work through me.
The mark of success is upon me!
I hold firm to this idea and rededicate and
reconsecrate myself to letting that true
Self express Itself and work through me.
My new good is now being prepared for me.
I give life the Light touch! I go with the
flow of Spirit, and I am grateful.

One or more of these lines may speak to you in a special way. If so, concentrate on that sentence, and affirm it for yourself, for it resonates with something deep within you. It will begin to work in you from the inside out, bringing forth that inner strength to your outer affairs.

The twenty-first century is about moving from self-improvement to Self-awareness—to functioning from the awareness that you truly are a part of something greater.

If we are to survive and succeed in this coming century of unparalleled transformation, we will have to work from this inner awareness of our spiritual Self-identity and Self-worth.

In past decades the powerful Self-Image Reinforcement Cycle was the main driving force behind the popular self-improvement movement. It was used to explain the workings of our subconscious phase of mind and how to program it to improve our lives. It was the basis for popular goal-setting and mind-power workshops.

Unfortunately, the principles were mainly taught on the pop-psychology level and rarely touched on the higher spiritual level where the power of the true Self resides. It alone has the real power to transform our lives.

Review the following diagram of the Self-Image Reinforcement Cycle (Figure #1), and then apply its principles on the spiritual level to bring forth your true Self. The cycle begins with the image we hold of ourselves in our minds, which determines our performance and then cycles around to reinforce our opinion of our performance. This self-talk in turn confirms the image we hold of ourselves. Then the cycle begins all over again—keeping us captive to the cycle. A negative self-image reinforces failure, while a positive self-image reinforces success.

Figure #1   Self-Image Reinforcement Cycle

OUR SELF-IMAGE (stored in subconscious)
Example: Image of ourselves feeing insecure and inferior during job interviews or reacting unfavorably to authority figures.

Reinforces our SELF-TALK, our opinion of our performance. ("I knew I'd fail that interview; what did I expect?") This self-talk reinforces the poor image of ourselves—starting the cycle all over again.

Affects our PERFORMANCE: We actually perform poorly in job interviews or when faced with authority figures.

Subconscious Feedback Loop

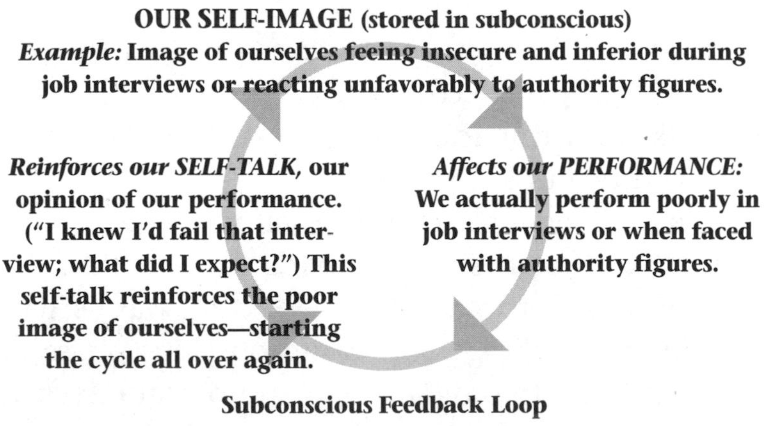

What goes around in our minds comes around in our lives.

Like a computer, our subconscious phase of mind is neutral and accepts any data programmed into it, regardless of whether the data is true or false, self-defeating or self-affirming. It does not question the data that we, our parents, or society have programmed into it. When we look at our lives, we can see what kind of data has been programmed into our subconscious computer. The old computer adage *garbage in, garbage out* applies here very well.

The "computer printout" shows up in terms of the situations in our lives, our health, relationships, and careers. For instance, if you are in a dead-end job that is not right for you, you may be saying to yourself subconsciously, "I can't see myself sitting here doing this for the rest of my life." This mental programming will cause you to leave voluntarily, get fired, or get sick so you won't have to do that work any longer. Interesting, isn't it?

My wife Marilyn felt this way about her first job right out of junior college. Working as an executive secretary in a large pharmaceutical firm, she actually became physically sick before she had the gumption to follow what she desired to be doing in life. That crisis broke her loose to return to college and begin preparing for her heart's desire—a career in teaching. Later, as she awakened to her true Self, she moved into the field of spiritual teaching and counseling and became a minister.

Below is an example of how the Cycle will operate to your advantage as you begin to function from your Higher Self:

Figure #2   Awareness of One's True Self

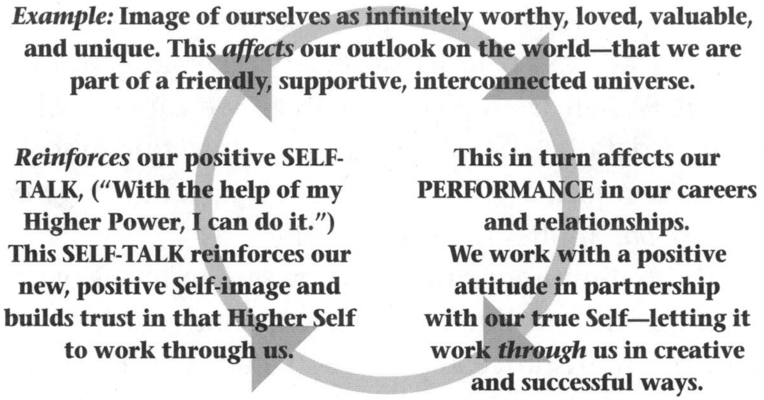

Example: **Image of ourselves as infinitely worthy, loved, valuable, and unique. This *affects* our outlook on the world—that we are part of a friendly, supportive, interconnected universe.**

Reinforces **our positive SELF-TALK, ("With the help of my Higher Power, I can do it.") This SELF-TALK reinforces our new, positive Self-image and builds trust in that Higher Self to work through us.**

This in turn affects our PERFORMANCE in our careers and relationships. We work with a positive attitude in partnership with our true Self—letting it work *through* us in creative and successful ways.

Feedback Loop

Working from your Higher Self, the Cycle will reinforce your self-confidence and you will be able to love and accept your human self in the midst of its struggles and mistakes. To know in your heart that you are worth loving, despite your shortcomings, is very empowering. It dissolves your fear and defensiveness.

Management statistics reveal that the single greatest cause of a worker's difficulty on the job and subsequent firing is not incompetence, but the inability of the individual to get along with fellow workers and superiors. It is their image of themselves as being unloved, unacceptable, or not measuring up that produces their sense of insecurity and defensiveness.

Whenever you catch yourself feeling defensive in a situation, silently remind yourself, "I don't have to feel defensive. I am a unique and valuable individual. I am capable and worth loving." (See Inner Activity #2.) Your Self-confidence will return and you will begin to react positively to people around you. You will be reconnecting with your Power.

EMPLOY YOUR POWER OF INNER VISIONING TO IMPACT THE SELF-IMAGE CYCLE

Everything in our lives originates with a picture held in our minds, which then acts as a magnet to gather emotional energy around it. That emotional energy—be it faith-based or fear-based—powers the process to bring the picture into form and manifestation.

Below is a brainstorming exercise to help you break loose from the limitations you have believed about yourself and then visualize your life as you truly desire it to be. *What vision are you holding for yourself and your life—the best or the worst?*

As you complete the exercise—let the answers flow from your heart, not your head. In order to tap into your intuitive, right-brain nature, write the answers with your nondominant hand.

Ask your Inner Counselor to help you.

Inner Activity #3 · Personal Visions

Ask yourself, "How would I really like to see myself (in terms of career, health, family, relationships, etc.)?" The best would be—

to see myself working as (describe) _____

to see myself as being _____

to see myself expressing _____

to see myself having _____

to see myself receiving _____

to see myself living _____

to see myself doing _____

to feel _____

to know _____

to _____

Visualize yourself being, expressing, and so on, according to those ideas. Let your prayer be—

"Thank You, Inner Partner,
for bringing forth the best that is within me."

Add the power of your feelings to your visualizing. Begin to feel yourself *being* this new person. Ask yourself, "What would it feel like to be . . . ?" Contemplate this. Involve your five senses to make it as real as possible to your subconscious—not only visualizing, but hearing the sounds of it and involving your body by acting it out in free interpretative movements. How would your inner child act it out?

In the language of computer electronics, you are making it "virtual reality." Electronic simulator programs are so real that you feel you can reach out and touch objects or walk through scenes.

These devices are electronic counterparts of what we can create with our own vivid imaginations and strong feelings. On the screen of our minds, we can create a realistic picture of whatever we earnestly desire. Our subconscious receives the image and uses the emotional energy we feel about the image to make it a reality in our lives.

In a later chapter you will have an opportunity to make use of this same principle by constructing a visual prayer chart to visualize your right new work.

The most powerful way to use the Cycle is to invite the Original Programmer to bring forth the Original You.

Your Creator has placed a perfect operating system at the core of your being. You are programmed for life, love, joy, and success. Through ignorance and fear you have overridden this original program and entered self-defeating data. Society has slipped "viruses" of failure and confusion into your system.

In your quiet time of prayer and meditation, ask your wise and loving Creator to erase and replace this wrong programming and to bring forth the confident Self that is your true nature.

Unity co-founder Charles Fillmore's "Invocation" is a beautiful prayer to use for this purpose:

I am now in the presence of pure Being,
and immersed in the Holy Spirit of life, love,
and wisdom.

I acknowledge Thy presence and Thy
power, O blessed Spirit; in Thy divine wisdom
now erase my mortal limitations and from Thy
pure substance of love bring into manifestation
my world, according to Thy perfect law.[2]

The sacred name of your Higher Self is "I Am."
This is the secret name of God within each of us, as
revealed to Moses in his mystical "burning bush" experience. In his inner dialogue with God, Moses
asked to know God's name. He was told: "I AM THAT
I AM . . . . This is my name for ever" (Exod. 3:14–15
ASV).

Whenever we use this "I Am," we are saying, "I
Am that—." Therefore, *whatever ideas we connect with
the power of that name will produce accordingly in our
life—either to our benefit or our disadvantage.* Unfortunately, we use the name unknowingly and wrong-
fully every day.

How many times do we hear people say, "I am
sick and tired of . . ." or "I am burned up about . . ."
or "I am a failure"? Do not take the Lord's name in
vain by using it in connection with self-defeating
thoughts.

The name should only be used in connection with
positive ideas that express your higher potential, such
as I Am capable, I Am wise, I Am that which I desire

to be! I Am That! Remember, your subconscious rec-ognizes and responds to your own voice more than any other; your voice is your subconscious's "voice of authority." Your subconscious accepts your voice's input without question and works to obey.

As you meditate on the following I Am statements, you will be calling to mind the ideal qualities of your true nature and programming powerful instructions into your subconscious.

This list is adapted from Dana Gatlin's book *God Is the Answer*:

I Am strong—staunch, sane, substantial!
I Am whole—happy, harmonious, healthy!
I Am alive—quickened, awake, alert!
I Am free—unbound, untrammeled, soaring!
I Am glad—buoyant, vibrant, resilient, grateful!
I Am true—untarnished, flawless, radiant!
I Am unafraid—courageous, dauntless, reliant!
I Am secure—poised, confident, assured!
I Am kind—useful, cheerful, friendly!
I Am big-hearted—magnanimous, generous, forgiving!
I Am able—competent, willing, dependable!
I Am sustained—unassailable, invulnerable, undefeat-able! [3]

Add your own ideas to the list. Here are a few sug-gestions for creating your own I Am statements:

I Am one with the Infinite Abundance of God.
I Am abundantly and appropriately supplied by the rich substance of God.

I Am serenely confident and Christ-assured.
I Am strong and whole and always will be.
I Am _____

As you hold these statements in mind, use "virtual reality"—visualize being that quality, and add the power of your feeling nature. Feel yourself being strong, capable, and so forth. Feel the joy and gratitude of being each quality. Act as if it were a reality. This is what makes it real.

Remember, the subconscious does not know the difference between an imagined experience and an actual one. It will work to produce whatever it is given as input.

Use the power of your conscious breathing to implant these statements into your mind. Your breathing directly accesses your subconscious mind and serves as a carrier wave to implant these ideas and feelings. As you slowly and consciously inhale and exhale, mentally speak the I Am statements.

For example, slowly and deeply breathe in on "I Am," hold for a moment, and shift your attention to your heart (the center of power), and picture yourself strong and capable. Then breathe out on the words, "strong and capable." Repeat this several times until you really feel it take root within your heart.

In the ancient Gaelic Christian tradition, there is an anonymous prayer that helps us to know there is something much greater living and working in us and empowering us. Pray it and feel newly connected with that Source within you:

O Christ, Thou Son of God,

My own eternal Self,

Live Thou Thy life in me,

Live Thou Thy love in me,

Do Thou Thy will in me,

Be Thou made flesh in me,

I will have no will but Thine,

I will have no self but Thee.

I like to pray it, adding a phrase to the third and fourth lines: "Until there is no more me, and only Thee." This further surrenders our outer transitory self and merges us with that true Self within us. You may wish to pray the prayer in this way.

As you let this powerful prayer work in you, the old, false programming begins to dissolve, and the right and true, original programming begins to surface. You begin to live from this Higher Self. You begin to live from the *inside out!* Your life takes on a new radiance and confidence you have never known before, and you will carry that confidence into your work experience.

You will begin to believe in the worth of your own ideas as coming from that Inner Wisdom working through you. Emerson explains this eloquently in his classic essay "Self-Reliance." Read it once a year to remind yourself of your own worth and power.

> To believe your own thought, to believe that what is true for you in your private heart is true for all men—that is genius. . . . A man should learn to detect and watch that gleam of light which flashes across his mind from within, more than the lustre of the firmament of bards and sages. Yet he dismisses without notice his thought, because it is his. In every work of genius we recognize our own rejected thoughts; they come back to us with a certain alienated majesty. . . .
>
> Insist on yourself; never imitate. Your own gift you can present every moment with the cumulative force of a whole life's cultivation; but of the adopted talent of another you have only an extemporaneous half possession. That which each can do best, none but his Maker can teach him.[4]

SECOND BLOCK:
Dissolving Resentment and Unforgiveness

The single greatest cause of unhappiness and troubled careers is the resentment and unforgiveness that we carry from childhood, family, and career experiences.

I had insights into the effect of these hidden factors during a visit to friends who lived in a lovely farmhouse in the Blue Ridge Mountains of Virginia. When we arrived, my friend Angelo was down on his knees under the bathroom sink, struggling with a pipe connection.

When he came up for air, he showed me a corroded old pipe he had just replaced. It was so badly clogged with mineral deposits that only a small trickle of water could flow through it. As I looked at the pipe, I thought of the pipelines in our body—the veins and arteries—and how they become clogged with cholesterol and fatty deposits that restrict the flow of life-giving blood.

In similar ways, our "spiritual arteries," our lifelines to our Creator's love and wisdom, can become so badly clogged with resentments, old hurts, and unforgivenesses that the flow of good into our lives is severely restricted. There is no way to perform a "heart bypass" on them. They must be dissolved before we can function successfully in our right work expression.

IDENTIFY THE BLOCKS AND ADVERSARIES

The first step in dissolving these blocks and adversaries is to find out whom and what we are resenting or fearing—whom and what we are viewing as an adversary. Many of these may lie just below the surface of our conscious awareness.

Clustering can help you identify these adversaries. In this technique, ideas branch off from a central theme, bringing forth insights from our inner feelings and beliefs.

Following is a sample of clustering ideas around the central theme of "I give up."

Figure #3   **Clustering "I Give Up" Ideas**

Inner Activity #4   Clustering

For your own clustering diagram, take a sheet of paper and in the center write this phrase:

What's holding me back?

Draw a circle around it. Now just brainstorm at random—letting ideas and feelings spin off from that central idea, each one with an arrow leading to another idea. You'll get some real surprises, some real "Ah-ha's."

Next, do a second cluster around this question:

Who is the adversary?

Take a few quiet moments to close your eyes and silently ask yourself this question. See what adversaries pop into your mind—bosses, authority figures, relationships, home, work. Scan back to your childhood and teen years, your family members, neighbors.

Let old feelings surface that have been buried for a long time. Which ones still touch a sore spot and make you feel like a victim or as though you have been unjustly treated? Which ones evoke feelings of anger, resentment, hurt, guilt, self-condemnation?

When you have identified "who," create a third cluster around that particular name which still stirs a negative feeling in you. Let your thoughts and feelings about that person spin off and branch out.

Now that you have found what is holding you back and who is involved in your resentment and unforgiveness, you can set about releasing yourself from those feelings by using the following method:

THE FREEDOM AND RELEASE LETTER

This proven method for dissolving and releasing these old blocks came to me in meditation some years ago to help me dissolve some strong resentments I was carrying concerning a business situation. It worked so well that I began to give the method to people who came to me for counseling. It always freed them, regardless of how far in the past the resentment or hurt had occurred. Conflicts, stalemates, and career delays would fade away.

We cannot move into our new right work expression until we have healed the negative feelings we may be carrying about our former jobs or employers. We only bring them with us into the new job. These feelings stand like gray ghosts barring the door to our success.

This was the case with a man employed as a city manager for a small city. He was a capable, outstanding executive, and was well liked by the citizens of the community, who appreciated his efforts to improve their city.

Unfortunately, he was bucking up against a city council that was tightly controlled by an "old boys" faction which jealously thwarted his best projects. Finally, during a stormy public council meeting, the controlling faction made false accusations against him and pressured enough votes to ask for his resignation.

The man was understandably hurt and resentful of the injustice and harm to his reputation. His first reaction was to want to bring suit against them, but in a quiet time of reflection, he realized that he truly wanted to be free of the entire dirty affair. To bring suit, even though he had an excellent chance of winning, would only entangle him in a long, drawn-out court battle that would hold him back from moving on to his new work.

He worked through the forgiveness process contained in the Freedom and Release Method and was able to clear himself of the resentment and negative feelings. Equally important, he gained the valuable insight that there was too much politics inherent in a city manager's position. He could better serve his purpose of helping communities to grow by being in the position of a director of economic development.

Freed of his blocks of negativity and aided by this new insight, he began his search. In a few months, working with his Inner Employment Counselor, he was led into just such a position. The new job also offered the added advantage of being located near the home of his ailing, elderly parents, who were of major concern to him.

Sometimes the hidden factors blocking us are further back in our past, all but forgotten, but they are still generating negative energy that carries over into our present work and relationships.

The Freedom and Release Method will help you dissolve these and open the pathway ahead of you.

A woman found this method helpful to overcome delays in the sale of her home. She had made plans to return to Ireland to care for her ailing mother, as well as to fulfill her career desire of opening a bed-and-breakfast inn overlooking the ocean.

Unfortunately, her home was not selling, although she had done everything in outer ways to sell it—had painted it, had made it very attractive, had lowered the price, and so forth. The deadline for her leaving the country was getting very close when she came in for counseling.

In the course of our talking and meditating together, she discovered a forgotten resentment and grief connected with a man she was engaged to marry some time ago. They were to have lived in that home together, but the relationship had broken up before their marriage became a reality. Unconsciously she was connecting letting go of the house with the letting go of her hopes for marriage.

In prayer and meditation she was able to visualize the person and extend forgiveness to him. As she released him into God's care, she was able to release her emotional attachment to the home as well.

The next day she called excitedly to say that she had a buyer for the house and that settlement would come just before she was to leave for Northern Ireland! The hidden delay had been dissolved, and she went forward with a light heart and renewed faith.

In your own situation, you may feel you have been deeply hurt, wronged, or misused by someone. Or perhaps you are feeling guilty that you have hurt someone and need to ask for, and receive, their forgiveness.

In every situation the healing depends upon releasing our own feelings and reaching a point of true forgiveness and understanding. We can only heal our own negative feelings and reactions; we cannot control the other person's.

Thus, we have the power to bring peace to ourselves, because we are in charge of the forgiveness process. It does not depend on the other person involved. It is the greatest act of self-empowerment that we can give to ourselves.

This forgiveness method was used successfully by a young woman working in a small job that did not make use of her greater talents. She had previously worked at a much higher-level job. She had sent out many resumes and had searched the job market, but to no avail.

During our counseling session, it was soon apparent that she was in a very negative emotional state stemming from the breakup of her marriage. She was in the middle of divorce proceedings, and she was full of resentment toward her husband. Her resentment and unforgiveness was like a gray energy field that surrounded her in every job interview. Her invisible negativity spoke louder than anything she could say to the interviewer.

She saw the importance of letting her resentments go and used this method to free herself of the negative feelings. Within a few weeks she was called to a job in a promising career in marketing.

The dramatic effectiveness of the Freedom and Release Letter lies in its thorough clearing of all four levels of our nature—physical, emotional, mental, and spiritual.

The method is constructed in such a way that each aspect of our nature, starting with the lowest and working up to the highest, is successively brought into the clearing and releasing process. Each step clears the way for the one that follows. The steps are cumulative. In order for the letter to be effective, please do not skip any steps. The letter is not actually mailed, but instead, in the final step, is burned in a freeing and releasing activity.

Inner Activity #5   Freedom and Release Letter

FREEDOM

RELEASING
the ceremony of releasing to God
5th STEP (Spiritual)
FORGIVING
exchanging the negative for the positive view
4th STEP (Spiritual)
AFFIRMING THE TRUTH
you no longer have to be a victim of this situation
3rd STEP (Mental–Spiritual)
DIALOGUING
gaining insights into what triggered your reactions
2nd STEP (Intellectual–Intuitive)
VENTING
getting your negative feelings "off your chest"
1st STEP (Physical–Emotional)

The Freedom and Release **Letter** leads us through the sequence of five simple steps outlined in the above diagram. Begin at the **bottom** step.

First Step—Venting

Before we can bring ourselves to the point of forgiveness, we must first let our personal ego "have its say."

Like a hurt child, it wants to cry, pout, demand revenge, or throw a temper tantrum. It is prideful and resists any attempt at true forgiveness. True forgiveness is completely contrary to the ego's belief that revenge is always justified; true forgiveness is a threat to the ego's need to always maintain control.

Sometimes we try to put a prayer Band-Aid over the emotional wound without first cleansing it. We pray and pretend all is well, but underneath, our hurt ego is still feeling the pain. The wound festers in the dark recesses of our heart, and the peace of mind that we desire eludes us, despite our fervent prayers.

The problem is that we have not given our personal self an opportunity to vent its feelings, defend itself, demand justice, and feel sorry for itself.

Thus, the first step in clearing the negative emotions is to let our "unhappy child" express its fears, tears, anger, and hurt in a harmless way.

In this step we give ourselves a chance to discharge the toxic emotions that are poisoning our minds and bodies. We get them "off our chests"— out of our hearts, where they can do damage—and put them down on paper, where we can later look at them objectively.

As you prepare to do this now, stand back and observe your ego starting to squirm at having to write this step. It will throw up quite a smoke screen of excuses to talk you out of taking time to do this very important clearing process. It does not want to be found out, doesn't want to lose control. In its own insane way, it does not want to give up its feelings of anger, attack, self-justification, and pain.

It fears facing old hurtful situations and would rather not "talk about it." It may try to convince you that the situations are already "over and done with," and therefore do not need to be opened.

I once counseled someone who thought that way. She had already put a prayer Band-Aid on a painful situation, but she really had not faced her feelings about it. As it turned out, after we talked for a while, she wrote not one letter, but seven, going all the way back to childhood issues she had "stuffed" by pretending they did not exist.

If you still find yourself thinking about an unhappy experience—if the old movie is still playing in the back of your mind—then you know you are not free of it. It is still siphoning off your emotional energy and blocking your success.

Another delaying tactic of our ego is to tell us that our anger is justified—that we are in the right and the other person is in the wrong. This tactic prevents us from having to take responsibility for at least partially creating the situation.

So be conscious of the reasons why you do not want to write the first step. Ask yourself, "Are the reasons genuine, or are they just games my ego is playing so it does not have to face the clearing process?" Expect a little flak from your ego as you sit down to do this first step.

Take a sheet of paper and address it to the person or persons involved.

(It makes no difference whether or not they are physically alive on earth at this time, because on the soul energy level you are still connected emotionally and spiritually and their soul will receive the message.)

The deeper meaning of this process is that on the inner levels of our being we are all connected with each other. The thoughts and emotions we radiate affect everyone else. This connection is especially strong with people with whom we have exchanged strong emotional energy, love, fear, resentment, jealousy, anger, and so forth.

At the time of the difficulty, we were transmitting and exchanging negative energy. This energy was stored in the subconscious—in the cells of the body. Scientifically, negative emotions actually change the body's chemical balance and the internal secretions that affect the immune system, and these changes lead to breakdown and disease.

Resentment, self-pity, and unforgiveness are especially detrimental to the body's health. Dr. Loring T. Swaim, formerly of the Harvard Medical School, conducted a 25-year case study on rheumatoid arthritis sufferers. He found that "resentment is one of the most powerful of human emotions, akin to anger and hate. It is persistent—fed by contact, association, memory, and imagination. It upsets the normal balance of the internal secretions and of digestion. . . . My belief is that chronic harmful emotions are a primary factor in the onset and the development of rheumatoid arthritis. . . . *Permanent release from harmful emotions can come only through 'change.'*

"Spiritual change apparently has an effect on rheumatoid arthritis similar to that of ACTH and cortisone, although the response is not so immediate. But while these hormones bring relief only while being taken, spiritual change removes some basic disturbing factor that has upset the entire body, and the improvement is lasting."[5]

There was a definite and significant improvement in the condition of those patients whom he could persuade to forgive themselves and the people in their lives they had been resenting, and to release their resentment to God. In many cases the condition was totally healed. It is this mind/body connection that makes writing these letters so healing for ourselves. When we write them to the other person involved, we are really writing to that aspect of ourselves which they represent in us.

In completing the forgiveness process, we not only heal ourselves and the other person on the soul level, but we also help heal the entire human race consciousness, for we are all one on the universal level.

The forgiveness process releases the aggregation of negative energy that has been held captive by our self-condemnation and guilt. When we forgive, the captive energy is suddenly neutralized and we feel newly empowered and free.

Begin your letter this way: "Dear (*person's name or your own,*)."

You may choose to write a letter to yourself. This is important because we usually have things for which we need to forgive ourselves, such as self-condemnation, guilt, and regrets.

Now pour out all your feelings on the first page. Don't hold back. Honestly and frankly describe how you feel—unjustly treated, angry, put down, abandoned, sad, guilty, and so forth.

Let your sentences begin with "I feel," rather than "I think." This shifts you out of your head and into your heart, where feelings are stored.

After you have vented your feelings in this first step, your emotions will have calmed down to the point where you can begin to think rationally and gain some insights on the entire situation. You are now ready for the second step.

SECOND STEP—DIALOGUING

Remember, we are never upset for the reasons we think; a situation is always pushing some hidden buttons. Dialoguing is a way to look at both sides of a situation, find the buttons, and bring forth needed insights and understanding.

1. Write these questions: "What made me react the way I did? What old memories, guilts, fears, and emotional scars from the past triggered my reactions? Am I seeing this situation through the glasses of those past traumas? Do they really apply to this present sit-

uation? Are they still valid today? Am I still the same person I was back then? Am I not a different person now?"

After you have written these questions, close your eyes and let the answers flow through your mind onto your paper. To deepen the effectiveness, try writing with your left or nondominant hand (as the case may be).

I know this sounds strange and will feel clumsy, but as you persevere in forming the letters, you are keeping your left, logical brain occupied, leaving an opening for your right brain/intuitive nature to express itself. People have been amazed at what comes forth from this other-handed/nondominant writing!

The heart empties out its feelings through the hand. Let your anger, grief, and resentment drain out through your hand onto the paper.

During this time you may get in touch with your own hidden buttons—find old emotional traumas and receive some "Ah-ha's" on why you reacted the way you did. This may lead you to write the letter to yourself to forgive and release self-anger and self-hate.

2. Write these questions: "What old hurts, fears, and defense mechanisms might have prompted this person to act as he/she did? What does the situation look like from his or her viewpoint—through the other person's own hurts and emotional glasses?"

Again, close your eyes and listen quietly to any answers that come to you, and write with your nondominant hand. Take your time, and let the new understandings flow.

As you gain insights into why the other person acted in such a way, you may find that you were both acting from similar fears. You may both be suffering from the same pain, mirroring it back to each other.

One man who used this process found that he was able to see into the pain of his father, who had beaten and abused him as a child. He saw that his father was passing along the same pain he himself had experienced as a boy at the hands of his own fear-ridden father. Through the process of forgiveness and release on the soul level, this individual was able not only to free himself from the bondage of the resentment, but also to free the souls of his father and grandfather as well. Three generations!

THIRD STEP—AFFIRMING THE TRUTH

Now that you have gained a new understanding about yourself and the other person in the situation, you can rise above the limited consciousness of the problem and affirm the spiritual Truth about yourself.

Write: *"The Truth about me is that I do not have to feel threatened or afraid. I have the power to choose how I will react.*

"I am no longer a victim of this situation, for I am in command of my choices. I choose to free myself from the negativity of this situation.

"I have the power to forgive and reimage this situation

and see it harmonize and work out for the highest good of all concerned. I now see it from the standpoint of my new understanding."

After you have written the above statements, speak them aloud.

FOURTH STEP—FORGIVING

Having vented the old emotions and gained new understanding about both sides of the issue, you are now ready for the actual forgiving and releasing activity. This step cannot be done successfully until the previous steps have prepared the way.

What does true forgiveness mean? Break the word into two parts: *for-give*—for giving up, letting go in exchange for—. Examples: I am for giving up pain in exchange for peace. I am for giving up and letting go of my old, limited erroneous views of the situation, in exchange for seeing from a higher understanding and perspective.

1. Close your eyes and mentally picture the person standing in a spotlight of God's radiant light, and write: "I forgive you for not understanding me. Please forgive me for not understanding you. The forgiving love of Jesus Christ (or my Higher Power) now dissolves all past inharmonies. This situation is being harmonized right now, as Spirit directs. You are free and I am free. I release you to your good. Please release me to mine. Go in peace."

2. Now mentally picture yourself releasing the entire situation and everyone concerned to God, to

harmonize and adjust for the highest good of all concerned. It may help to imagine yourself dumping it all into the fast-flowing, crystal-clear stream of God's pure love, to be dissolved.

3. Finally, write:

"Thank You, God, for perfect freedom and a perfect outworking, according to Thy loving will for the highest good of all concerned. Amen." Take a deep breath, and as you exhale, release the entire situation.

FIFTH STEP—RELEASING

Your Freedom and Release Letter is now complete. However, you can deepen the effect of your forgiving and releasing by finishing with an ancient purification ritual. Since prehistoric times, fire has always been a symbol of purification. It is imbedded in our caveman nature.

Use this powerful symbol of fire now, and burn your letter in a fireplace or in a bowl lined with silver foil. As you touch the flame to the letter, pray a final prayer of release, seeing the negative emotions purified and dissolved. Release it all to God. It is finished. You are free. You will begin to experience a new peace and well-being.

On the higher spiritual level, the activity of God will continue to work to bring about a deeper understanding as the old, negative energy blocks dissolve. What has now been accomplished on the inner realms will work its way outward and bring resolution in due course.

Leave it all in God's hands, and go peacefully about your business. If it should come into your mind again, simply bless it and give it back to God to handle. Affirm: *"Peace! Be Still!"* *God is in charge.* You are free of it, and your pathway is clearing before you.

Third Block:
Letting Go of Old Roles and Identities

After working in a career for many years, we often become very attached to that old career role. It becomes who we are—our persona with which we meet the world. It is our armor, our security blanket. Without it we have "nothing to wear." We feel naked and unsure of ourselves.

At social gatherings, one of the first things people ask in getting acquainted is, "What do you do?" Immediately our persona, and the importance of who we are, is narrowed down to our occupation. It is the basis of their judgment of our self-worth, our identity.

If we are out of work or retired, suddenly we no longer have any status or identity. All the importance of who we were is gone. We no longer have that work image to give us worth or to hide behind.

In our American workaholic culture, with its emphasis on the work ethic for status and acceptance, to be out of the work stream can be very traumatic. Many people grieve and experience serious health challenges after they let go of their power roles.

This feeling is especially traumatic if we are a workaholic and dependent upon our work to give us self-worth.

Our insecure little ego asks, "Well, if I am not that person anymore, if I am not clothed in that role anymore, then who *am* I?"

If you are experiencing this type of identity crisis right now, rejoice, for it can yield a great blessing for you. It will force you to examine just who you really are!

For the first time in your life, you may actually stop what you are doing, take your nose off the grindstone, and look around at yourself and your purpose in life. This interlude out of the work stream can be a powerful time for you to discover your true identity.

It will force you to search deep within yourself—beyond the work clothes—to get in touch with the real Self of you—the one that transcends any outer persona.

Suddenly you may awaken to the great Truth that you are something more than your body, your personality, your cultural and vocational identity. The great and scary and wonderful idea dawns that you are an eternal, spiritual being with unlimited potential to fulfill many roles. Suddenly you are put to the test of trusting the loving and Creative Mind that originally endowed you with your talents and allowing It to provide for you.

You begin to realize that any temporary role you

play in life is only a means to express your greater role, that of being a co-creator with Creative Intelligence.

Let go of "who you used to be," so that you can step into the new role that your Inner Partner is preparing for you in which you can serve in a more meaningful way than ever before. Your anxiety will dissolve as you understand that the responsibility to find your right work is not yours, but your Inner Partner's. It is in your Partner's best interest to move you into the work that It wishes to accomplish through you. Your job is to simply get your fears and blocks out of the way and listen. Stop fretting and start letting!

The Mind that created you knows the "how" and will guide and provide for you. Do not try to figure out how it will come about nor try to manipulate results with your intellect. The "how" is not your concern.

Relax; stay open and receptive to changes. Whatever feels "light" is right. Dark feelings are a sign that you are off course and need to reconnect consciously with the Source.

Here are some positive statements to strengthen your faith. Select a few that really speak to you. Memorize them so that you can call them to mind to counter any worry thoughts which assail you during the day or night.

SPIRIT-LIFTERS

The Mind that created me loves me still and has a plan for me which is better than anything I can envision for myself.

The Mind that brought me this far will guide me safely the rest of my way. I go with the flow of Spirit.

I am willing to release the former me and step out on faith to bring forth the new me.

I have faith in God to open ways where, to human sense, there appears to be no way.

New opportunities and new avenues of prosperity are opening for me now, and I am grateful.

No person, situation, or economic condition can keep my good from me.

I can hardly wait to see the new good that God has for me.

You may want to type selected statements and place them where you can see them—at your desk, on your refrigerator, or on your bathroom mirror. Carry a favorite one on a small card, as "Pocket Prayer Power" to remind you and lift you throughout the day.

POCKET PRAYER POWER

God has need of me and is right now preparing my right new work for me. Thank You, God.

> **POCKET PRAYER POWER**
>
> Trusting and resting,
> I place myself and all my affairs
> in God's loving care and all is well.
> Thank You, God.

When the voice of self-doubt in the back of your mind begins its litany of "what if's" and begins to paint negative scenarios, let these prayers be a countering litany. Repeat them silently until you feel your confidence restored.

Make a cassette recording of the prayer statements you have selected, with a background of soft meditative music. Play the tape as you fall asleep, so the ideas will program into your subconscious during the night. Play the tape around the house or while driving.

FOURTH BLOCK: Overcoming the Fear of Change and Its Consequences

Shakespeare was right when he wrote, "Our doubts are traitors, / And make us lose the good we oft might win / By fearing to attempt."[6]

The doubts we have about making a change or starting something new stand in the way of our good.

Here is a list of common fears relating to fear of change. See which ones resonate with your present situation:

- Fear of leaving the comfort and security of my present work, even if I am unhappy in it.
- Fear of loss of income from changing work.

- Fear of beginning something new and failing (a major cause of procrastination).
- Fear of succeeding and its accompanying responsibility.
- Fear of stepping out into the unknown, of taking a risk.

These fears are rooted in our ego's never-ending struggle for security. Security is the ego's Holy Grail. Our personal self views any change as a threat to its safety and control—and certainly job and career changes are major threats. They score high on the stress scale. You cannot move forward into your new work until you are willing to go with the flow of change so that you can receive its hidden blessing.

Below is a diagram of the *Insecurity Reinforcement Cycle,* which closely parallels the *Self-Image Reinforcement Cycle* shown in Figure 1. It depicts the ego's need to control. On some level of our lives, most of us are "control freaks"!

Figure #4	Insecurity Reinforcement Cycle

My fears of being unaccepted, alone, and unsure of myself create—

The more I try to keep things under control, the more I fail and the more insecure and frustrated I feel, which only reinforces my fear.

—a deep need for me to keep everything and everyone under my control, so I can feel more secure.

My attempts to control are futile, since everything in life is continually changing and since it is impossible for me to keep everything under control.

The participants in one of my workshops brain-stormed their feelings about the following statement:

"I need to control (situations, people, events) because . . ." (complete the sentence)
—I feel afraid I will lose something I have.
—I feel afraid I will lose something I want.
—I feel I should be in control.
—I feel I need to control the outcome because it gives me power over the uncertainties of life, the "slings and arrows of outrageous fortune."

—It makes me feel superior.
—It makes me a winner in life's game of winners and losers.
—It gives me an illusion of independence.
—I don't trust God.
—I don't trust others.
—I don't trust myself.

Which of these strikes a chord in you? What other feelings come to you? These will help you identify the hidden fears that need to be acknowledged and dissolved.

If we ever hope to evolve and move toward self-fulfillment, we must be willing to break out of our security perimeter, release our fears, and go with the flow of Spirit. Change is the only way that our Inner Partner can possibly move us into new good.

The Truth is that every change comes to us with a gift in its hands. Unfortunately, when we hold a negative attitude toward it, the gift appears to be wrapped in unattractive paper. Learning to see change as an instrument for our growth is one of our prime assignments in this school called "Earth."

A friend of ours, Paul McMillian, is a professional nature photographer. He and his wife Roberta gave us a large framed picture of a very dramatic storm scene that Paul photographed in the mesa country of the Southwest. It depicts a lone mesa towering against a dark sky and being battered by a huge thunder and lightning storm. The mesa stands naked but undaunted.

At the bottom of the picture Paul wrote: "Storms: Are they coming, or are they going? In the coming they bring new life; in the going they bring rainbows."

It is a powerful picture that speaks to me every time I look at it. It reminds me that when the storm-changes of life come to us, we are to stand undaunted, knowing that new blessings and new opportunities spring forth in their wake. Every change, even those that seem so traumatic, hide rainbows in them.

Whenever we are experiencing the chaos of change in our life, it is a sign that the old is breaking up to make way for new and greater good. Chaos is order in motion. This outer breakup is always frightening to our human self, which fears the cracks in its eggshell—its ego armor. We are like the egg that was afraid to hatch, which ended up going rotten inside. Either we dare to hatch out or we die inside.

On my desk, I keep a small clay sculpture of a baby turtle breaking out of its shell. With its flippers it is doing the breast stroke, pushing its shell away behind it. Its neck is sticking out, and it is looking up with a quizzical smile on its face. It is a reminder to me that if we are to break out of our security shell and move forward in life, we must push the past behind us, have the courage to stick our necks out, and face the future with a smile! It's time to break out of your shell and go for the good that God has for you!

Change, then, is a friend! Do not make an adversary of it. When we fear or resist it, we lose the opportunity to receive the blessing hidden in the change. We set the powerful law of cause and effect, sowing and reaping, into motion against us, and we always come out the loser.

Jesus, the Master, taught us how to handle change when he said:

"Agree with thine adversary [the change that you are resisting] quickly, whiles thou art in the way with him; lest at any time the adversary deliver thee to the judge, and the judge deliver thee to the officer, and thou be cast into prison" (Mt. 5:25 KJV).

Jesus is advising us to find the point of positive agreement with the change, lest our resistance and resentment deliver us to the "judge" (the law of cause and effect), which will "sentence" us to be a prisoner of the negative aspects of the change. Our negative attitude is the cause, and the delays and difficulties are the resulting effects.

The longer we hold on to a negative attitude about change, the longer we stay imprisoned in the negative aspects of the situation.

Our resistance to the troublesome changes in our life sets off a chain reaction, a domino effect, the end of which may have far-reaching negative effects down the road of life. You can make the domino effect work to your advantage by finding the point of agreement in the change. This will set into motion a new chain of positive results for you.

As you choose to agree with the change and find the good in it, you may see that the old job and the former boss actually did you a tremendous favor.

Looking back, you will be able to say: "I was in that job so long, I must have been hypnotized. I was in a rut. If someone hadn't kicked me out or made it uncomfortable for me to stay, I never would have moved on to my greater good."

This was the awareness that finally came to a man named Bob, who came to me for counseling. He had just been laid off from his job as circulation manager for a local daily newspaper. He told me that over the past years he had worked his way up through the various departments at the newspaper, and now in his forties, with a wife and two children and a mortgage, he was facing a major crisis.

After we used some of the methods outlined in

this book, he was able to shift his view of the situation and see it as a great opportunity to make a new start at what he always wanted to do—run his own newspaper.

We immediately began praying for his right new work, using the "Prayer for Right Expression" at the end of this section (Inner Activity #6). I explained to Bob that the prayer includes the essential point of surrendering our desires to our Senior Partner.

There is a difference between making something happen by the force of our mental will and letting our Higher Power bring it about. Forcing often brings unexpected, unwanted side effects.

The better way is to give the desire over to Higher Wisdom to bring about the best results. Working in this way gives us serenity and recharges our energy instead of depleting it.

Not long after our time together, Bob came to me with a great big grin on his face. An unusual opportunity had "just happened" to open up in a small town near where he had lived as a child. He was going to get his dream. The owner of the town's weekly newspaper was selling out, and Bob was able to arrange long-term financing.

All of Bob's experience, working up through the various departments in his previous company, would now be put to use in his new endeavor. The last I heard from him, the paper was doing fine, circulation was rising, and Bob and his wife were happily working together on their own weekly newspaper.

Ken was another executive who learned to view change as a blessing. Ken had experienced a very successful career track, serving as vice president in three different firms and successively moving up in salary benefits in each position.

However, at the last firm he had just settled in and was enjoying his new position when he ran into conflict with the president, who had just been hired. The new president's business ethics and motives were not of the highest, and since Ken would not go along with these lower ethics, the president made it very uncomfortable for him. Finally, Ken made the decision to leave the company. It was a painful and unsettling experience, and he was harboring much resentment about the entire situation.

In time, once his ego got over its negative reactions, Ken realized that the president had really done him a great favor. He was now free to move toward an even better position. With prayer and a new, positive attitude, he began to contact the finest companies in the business. In a short time he was called for interviews and hired as vice president of operations by a worldwide firm of the very highest reputation.

Another man was laid off from his work as an office manager. He took his situation into prayer and received the insight that this change was not a misfortune, but an opportunity to step out on faith and launch the dream he had been nurturing in the back of his mind. He wanted to begin a business on the Internet, a community-service Web site offering self-help information as well as related products to the growing number of people interested in spiritual growth and self-realization.

As he began working with the "Prayer for Right Expression," he overcame his initial fears about being out of work and was able to seek start-up capital. Within a few days of deciding to make his dream a reality, he was rewarded with backing from someone who believed in his project. It seemed a miracle to him, and I'm sure he would agree with the idea of "Menta-Miracles."

MENTA-MIRACLES

"Menta-Miracles" was a term coined by a close friend of mine, Alan Kamman, who travels all over the world in his work as a telecommunications consultant. During his lifetime he has experienced several career changes and challenges. In a letter to me, he described "Menta-Miracles":

"There are two things necessary to change your life for the better. One is a change in your mental attitude, and the second is positive prayer—which is your means of contacting the only Power that can bring about the miracle you desire.

"Miracles flow through open channels, like lightning bolts that follow a magnetic electrical path. Changing your attitude toward yourself and towards life creates the right magnetic path for the power of God to flow through."

Alan was stating an important formula: When we

combine a positive mental attitude with positive prayer power, we have an unbeatable combination. Use the following prayer to help you shift your mental attitude:

"I now claim the blessing this change holds for me. Show me the blessing, Lord. I welcome this change as a part of my spiritual unfoldment. It leads me to greater good. I can hardly wait to see the new good this change will bring for me."

It's as if the Inner Voice replies, "I thought you'd never ask! You were so busy grumbling and worrying, you never unwrapped My gift!"

Begin using the following prayer daily to open your mind to the guidance of your Inner Employment Counselor.

Inner Activity #6 Prayer for Right Expression

Holy Spirit,
I now let go of fear and doubt

and take hold of the divine idea that
there is good for me

and that I am being directed to my good right now.

I give thanks that You are already preparing

the right new work for my highest good

and that You are bringing this about in the right way,
at the right time, in the right place.

I give thanks that in this right new work

I will be abundantly prospered in the right way—
not only financially, but in the inner satisfaction

that I will be making the best use
of the talents and abilities

which You have given me to help and serve others.

I ask and give thanks in the full assurance

that this or something better is now being provided—

not according to *my* will, but in accordance with

Thy loving, wonderful will for my highest good.

My right work is opening to me now!

Trusting and resting, I place myself and all my affairs

in Thy loving care. Thank You, Spirit.

God is my Partner; I cannot fail! God is my Partner;
together we succeed!

Discovering Your Right Work

Chapter 3

Brainstorming New Career Possibilities

Now that you've cleared away the hidden blocks to expressing your true potential, you can begin to target your right and true work—that which you came to do in cooperation with your Senior Partner.

This may mean possibly bypassing your old work roles and even the "logical" employment moves. You are going for something much more fulfilling than you have ever done before—something which calls for your creative potential to be exercised, something which stirs the brain, lifts your spirit, and gets you out of bed in the morning eager to get to work!

Even if you are not sure of your right direction at

present, a few "loosening-up" exercises may help you to brainstorm the kind of work expression with which you can really resonate.

The following Inner Activities (#7, 8, and 9) will help you to break out of your old mind-set, so your Inner Partner can show you new possibilities.

Inner Activity #7 Checking Out Your Preferences

What appeals to you? Quickly circle your preferences.

I really love working with
—ideas
—people
—children
—animals
—nature, making things grow
—helping to heal people
—art
—music
—building things
—machinery, engineering
—creating, designing
—facts and figures
—managing, organizing
—wielding power
—being a mover and shaker
— _____
— _____

What working conditions and location would you prefer?

Think about your ideal working conditions.

—outside work or inside work?_____

—working at home, working away from home?

—what hours? _____

—travel time to work? _____

What hobbies or recreational activities do you love to do and have an aptitude for?

List _____

_____

_____

_____

Consider converting your hobbies and recreational interests into a new career.

A couple in their forties was experiencing burnout in their teaching careers. For relaxation they loved to garden and create beautiful plantings around their home in a northern state.

Together they took the time to pray about their careers, asking for direction. They were inspired to phase out their careers and enter the gardening and nursery business. Their prayers led them to a southern state, where they were able to buy partial interest in a nursery business that was failing. Seven years later they own the business entirely, and it is thriving.

Their nursery buildings and grounds are beautifully landscaped, and they have created a small lake and park that is often used for outdoor weddings. This couple had the courage to step out on faith and give their talents full expression, and their courage is paying off for them in inner satisfaction as well as outer success.

Turn Recreational Interests Into Careers

In your quiet time, look at your present recreational interests, as well as those that you enjoyed in childhood and your growing-up years. Which ones give or gave you a sense of satisfaction and accomplishment? These may provide clues for possible expansion into a career.

A young businesswoman owned a small, general-purpose sign-painting business that she operated out of her home. Although she showed some interest and aptitude for the work, she really had a deep love for sports, especially cross-country biking, scuba diving, surfing, and boating. When she brainstormed answers to Inner Activity #7, she realized that she could combine her business and sporting interests.

She began to specialize in sign making for sports shops. She solicited business from dive and surf shops, marinas, boat builders, and bicycle shops. She began to carve out a niche for herself, advertising in boating and biking business magazines.

She enjoyed rubbing elbows with surfing, boating, and biking enthusiasts, and soon earned a name for herself as the person to see for signs. Her business increased, and she really began enjoying her work as an extension of her recreational activities.

Inner Activity #8   "What Next, Lord?"

Try a few clustering exercises similar to the ones you did previously.

On a sheet of paper draw a circle around the question:

"What next, Lord?"

Invite your Inner Partner to do the brainstorming through you—spinning off new ideas you have not thought of yourself. You will be surprised at the possibilities that come through. One of them may be flashing a green light at you!

Try a cluster around the question:

"I want to be free to—"

Inner Activity #9   "The Sky's the Limit"

The purpose of this exercise is to lead you away from the past work histories and career roles you've always pictured yourself as performing. It serves to uncover desires and talents that may have never surfaced in your previous work experience.

As you complete the following "Sky's the Limit" sentence, let your playful self have fun with the possibilities. Don't let your ego tell you that they are "too good to be true." Let them blossom. Listen to your intuitive promptings as you write with your nondominant hand.

If I could do anything I wanted to do in life and had the energy, time, and resources to do it, I would really love to . . .
(complete sentence) _____

_____

_____

_____

You may have just written the seed idea of a new career. Explore the possibilities of it. Follow any leads that intersect your pathway. Be willing to follow your Inner Guidance.

The career ideas that may have popped out in these "loosening-up" exercises may be different from the work you originally pursued. This is because you have outgrown that work, just as you are outgrowing your old, limited consciousness.

As we grow spiritually, our values change. You may find yourself increasingly yearning for work that contributes to the well-being of people and of the Earth. You are in step with the new generation of individuals in the workforce who are working from higher motivation, beyond just making the biggest income possible. They want their work not only to have meaning but also to be of benefit to others.

In an earlier time, Henry Ford had service in mind when he decided to build a car that the working man could afford, instead of Cadillacs, Packards, and Pierce Arrows, which were only for the wealthy.

He applied himself to that idea and created the Model T Ford, a car that became part of the American dream. The original tin lizzies revolutionized this country. Every farmer and every factory worker had one, and later their sons had a "hot-rod Ford and a two-dollar bill" to take their girlfriends to the drive-ins.

The original Model T's were built by workers whom Ford hired at unheard-of wages—almost twice the pay offered anywhere else in the industry. He created a new prosperity in their meager lives, so they all could afford a car for their families. Their purchasing power blessed the local economy in manifold ways.

For Henry Ford's service to the average American, the Universal Mutual Support System made him a multimillionaire. He said, "The highest use of capital is not to make more money, but to make money do more for the betterment of life."[1]

I once heard an anecdote about Ford being called by one of the early dealers who wanted help in selling the cars. According to the story, Ford went out to visit the dealer and saw a big sign on the front of the dealership that said "SALES." Underneath it in small letters was the word *Service*. He told the dealer: "Change the sign to read in big letters SERVICE. Stop trying to push car sales, and start emphasizing how well you can serve your customers' needs."

The dealer took Ford's advice and his business started to flourish. *He understood he was not in the automobile business, but in the business of serving people.*

The business of serving others has never been better. It can bring you into exciting work that will bring joy to your heart and pay your rent as well. You will be happiest and most successful when your work benefits others, because service opens the way for your Senior Partner to work through you most effectively.

Open your mind to a career in one of the new industries that is just beginning to flourish. One of these careers may be "waiting in the wings" for you. It may not have been available during your previous work experience, but now—just as you are getting ready for a new expression—it breaks forth as a new possibility. These new careers combine making a profit with the higher priority of making a difference in the world.

Consider New Career Possibilities

Your interest may be sparked by one or more of these career ideas:

- Expansion of alternative-health professions, with their holistic approach to healing the whole person—Spirit, mind, and body. Dr. Larry Dossey and James P. Swyers wrote in "Alternative Medicine: Expanding Medical Horizons," a report to the National Institutes of Health in 1992:

"Americans appear to have made more total visits to practitioners of alternative medicine than to conventional primary care physicians—425 million visits versus 388 million—even though most of these visits to alternative practitioners were paid out of pocket . . . . Americans spent an estimated $13.7 billion on alternative therapies in 1990."[2]

Americans obviously are awakening to their three-fold nature and are desiring an integrated healing approach that addresses Spirit, mind, and body. *You* can be part of this holistic approach to wellness. It will take courage to leave your former career, but the rewards of being in your right work will more than make up for the struggle.

"Mary" worked in the traditional medical field for thirty years, finding less and less agreement with it every year. The steady income was high, but it came at a price of bouts with depression. Finally, she summoned the courage to step out on faith and trust her Senior Partner to provide for her as she trained to enter the field of alternative therapy.

She is now happier and freer than she has ever been, operating her own prospering healing practice.

- Education such as teaching and helping disadvantaged children, teens, and adults to escape the welfare track and make something of themselves. "Keith" is a successful lawyer who felt that he had outgrown his old work. He volunteered as a mentor in his local school system and enrolled in courses for a new career in the field of adult education. He is now on the faculty of his local adult-education system and finding new meaning and fulfillment in helping people to believe in their own worth and potential.
- Spirituality. Both the aging baby boomers and the thirty-something Generation X-ers are actively searching out new places to worship and study spiritual principles to apply in their work

and personal lives. If you have been involved in metaphysical and consciousness-raising studies, you may be feeling the call to enter formal training to become a teacher, workshop leader, or minister to serve this growing demand. If this is the case, nothing else will give you greater fulfillment.

- Environmental services and creative recycling. Responding to the grassroots pressures to save our planet, governments, corporations, and even the military have gone "green," opening up new job opportunities in this expanding field. In increasing numbers, corporations are now conducting environmental audits of their operations. Private entrepreneurs are also finding success in producing new products made from recycled materials.

You will also find a variety of fulfilling careers in the many not-for-profit foundations dedicated to saving the planet's environment, that is, The Nature Conservancy, the National Wildlife Federation, the Audubon Society, and the Sierra Club. Check your local library or Internet for a list of their corporate headquarters to contact.

- Employment overseas. The globalization of the world's economy has created unique opportunities abroad. Americans in record numbers are seeking their fortunes in foreign countries that offer unique advantages in lifestyles and culture. More than three million Americans now live abroad. This exodus is a major trend of the twenty-first century. The plus side of this migration is that it serves as a catalyst fostering international unity and peace. Research the countries carefully before you leap, but you could be heading into exciting and rewarding new work.

- Operation of retreat facilities in quiet places of natural beauty away from the noisy world. We live in a workaholic culture, and people need time away to recharge their batteries.

The American workaholic tendency has created a society of out-of-balance individuals who have no time for anything else. As a result, family life suffers and our inner selves suffer from malnutrition. People are yearning for meaningful ways to restore balance in their lives and feed their souls. The artificial entertainment of movies, TV, and spectator sports does not renew and revive us.

We need to reconnect with our ancient roots in the natural world. Nothing will heal us faster than quiet time spent in nature. There is something about the greenery and lakes and lofty mountains that strikes an ancient chord in our souls and restores our sanity. Satisfying this yearning is becoming a major industry.

New careers are opening in ecotourism—arranging and conducting "soft adventure" tours to the sacred places on earth, offering last-chance looks at endangered wildlife and scenic wonders.

- Temporary Services. Temp service agencies are growing fast in the United States today. Corporations are relying increasingly on part-time and "temp" staffing rather than carrying heavy payrolls of fully benefited full-time workers. Entrepreneurs are organizing their own temporary services agencies to meet niche situations that the regular employment agencies are not serving.

• Business ownership. If you are happy in your chosen field of expertise, consider making the break to go into business on your own—creating and marketing your own unique services and products that you can really believe in.

Home-business careers are becoming very sophisticated, with the advent of new computer technology, including the Internet, or World Wide Web. Over 14 million people now work full-time at home, and it is estimated that in the near future 44 percent of all households will support some sort of home business.

A successful former banking executive chose to create her own business. She and her partner conduct a thriving marketing-communications business from their homes. Although she lives in Connecticut and her partner in New Jersey, they stay in instant communication with each other by means of E-mail, fax, and FedEx as they prepare publicity and marketing material for corporations and mutual funds.

They have created a "virtual office" in cyberspace and they enjoy the added advantage of flexible work schedules as well. Their quick response-time to customer needs gives them a competitive edge over larger companies that are more cumbersome and less able to respond to the fast-changing market opportunities.

If a business at home is your guidance, your Inner Partner will give you the courage to launch out on your own and provide the openings and the resources for you. Like a newborn baby, every sincere desire of the soul comes forth from the Source, with the resources it needs for life already provided.

If your idea is a soul's sincere desire, it will succeed, because it is in line with the desire of your Senior Partner. We will be exploring this theme in the next chapter.

A Freeing Meditation

Here is a visualization meditation to help you break free of your old limitations:

Quiet yourself with a few deep, slow breaths— breathing in on the word *Peace* and out on the words *Be still*. Do this for a few minutes.

Now picture yourself sitting in a cramped position inside a box of limitation that is confining you. Take a deep breath and say to yourself:

"I am more than my limitations.
I am free by the power of my Indwelling Spirit."

Visualize yourself reaching up with your arms, pushing the lid off the box, and standing up. Push out the sides, and step free.

Declare: *"I am free and ready for my good! Praise God!"* Amen.

Feel your new freedom and potential. You have impressed a new message of freedom upon your subconscious. Repeat the meditation any time you feel boxed in by your limitations and self-doubts.

Chapter 4

Discovering Your Master Goal, Your True Purpose

The Inner Activities and meditation you have just completed were loosening-up exercises to stretch you beyond the limits of your old mind-set.

Now you are ready to gain deeper insights into your true purpose and the work you came to do and share. Whatever that work is, it will make use of the talents and abilities your Creator has endowed you with and provide an opening through which Spirit can be expressed.

This means that in whatever field of endeavor you are to function, there will be a Higher Work being accomplished through you as you go about your daily work.

The apostle Paul explained it well in his letter to the Philippians: "It is God who works in you to will and to act according to his good purpose" (Phil. 2:13 NIV).

Thus it is not *you* seeking, but God seeking to be expressed and to create *through* you. Your inner yearning is God knocking at the door of your consciousness—pressing to bring forth that which can only be done through you.

Thus we did not come into this world just to ricochet off the walls of circumstance. Each of us comes in with an assignment that is part of a larger plan. That assignment may lead us through many job experiences, but always and ever we are living out a larger purpose.

Every work experience is important in its own way at each point in our journey. It does not serve our best interests to resent any of them or to regret what appears to be past mistakes. Each has served a purpose that we may not be able to see until we gain a higher perspective.

The truth is that you would not have been ready for your right work previously. You did not have the consciousness nor the confidence you now possess. Rather than it being too late, it is now precisely the right time.

Right now, this very moment, beyond the scenes of your limited consciousness, you are on a converging course with your right and true work. It is being prepared for you, as you prepare yourself for it. Believe this and know it!

It is no coincidence that at this point in your life you are feeling the yearning to express your true talents and purpose. You are feeling the growing influence of the new consciousness forming as we enter the twenty-first century.

The new century will be one of unparalleled transformation. You need only to look at your own life and those around you to see the changes already happening—the breaking up of old patterns, making way for the new. The world is moving to a new and higher level of global functioning.

We are entering the Intuitive Age, and in this new era we will function intuitively, tapping into what I call the "Innernet."

Just as the Internet is a global network of electronic computer "brains," so there is a global Innernet—an intuitive network linking minds everywhere with the One Mind—Creative Intelligence. Each one of us is part of this new, planetary Innernet and has access through his or her quiet mind to its unlimited information.

British mathematician Peter Russell writes of this idea in his book *The Global Brain*. Russell suggests that "humanity is like some vast nervous system, a global brain in which each of us are the individual nerve cells. . . . Human society . . . can be seen as one enormous data-collection, data-communication, and data-memory system"[1]

As this global brain shifts to this higher, intuitive level of functioning, there will be a shifting of values from the materialistic philosophy of life that has brought so much trouble upon the world to a more holistic, spiritual perspective. In the twenty-first century we will be working from this new perspective of life.

In 1939 Charles Fillmore wrote prophetically: "The present turbulence in the world is the dissolution of the age of materialism. . . . The old order, like ice in a great river, is breaking up and is about to disappear."[2]

Indeed, the old order, with its authoritative corporate employment system, is already phasing out. The traditional career-planning model, with its aim of "womb-to-tomb" security and incremental promotions in one company or career, is finished. The former ways of gaining security no longer are working, if indeed they ever really worked. Nothing in the outer world can give us the security we seek.

The longer we live, the more we find that our only true security lies within our Self. Our success lies in tuning in to and trusting our Higher Wisdom and higher capabilities.

It is now time to trust that Higher Wisdom to lead you to your true purpose. Your Higher Self has led you to this point of readiness. It is now time to open your mind to that higher revelation.

The following meditative writing process will help you to discover your true purpose, your master goal. It is very powerful, because it brings your Higher Self into the discovery process.

The answers you receive will be uniquely for you. I cannot tell you what you will receive from Spirit, except that it will be of the *utmost importance* to you at this particular time in your life.

It will lead you out of your impasse and give you the encouragement to keep on keeping on. It will lead to a clearer understanding of what it is that you deeply desire to do and to be in this lifetime. Revealed will be the "song" you came into this world to sing.

Each of us has a song to sing, a song of creativity. It is unique with us. Just as no two melodies are exactly alike, so each person's own song of creativity and the expression of each person's talents cannot be imitated. We are not mockingbirds that imitate the songs of other birds. We came to sing our own songs, and we will only be happy when we find a way to express it.

My wife Marilyn has a prayer statement taped to her mirror that reminds her of this:

"No one and no thing can keep me from singing my Song–the Song my Soul came to sing. I sing it now and I rejoice! Praise God!"

In working with this seven-day process you will be letting faith through. You will be giving your Higher Power the green light. You will be giving God the go-ahead to work through you.

Set aside a very quiet time of day or night. If it means getting up before dawn when the house is quiet, do so.

Inner Activity #10   The 7-Day Discovery Process

For the first four days, ask yourself the following question. Use a separate sheet of paper for each day and be sure to date it.

Write: Beloved Indwelling Spirit, what is my highest aspiration—that which I came to fulfill?

After you have written the question, close your eyes and speak the question silently—and then aloud several times. Silently take the question into your heart and let it incubate there. As insights flow from Spirit, use your left or nondominant hand to write them down.

As you meditate and write on this same question each day, deeper insights will be revealed. Each succeeding day's writings will build upon the previous day's understanding and enrich and enlarge upon it.

For the final three days, write and meditate on the following questions (again using your left or nondominant hand to write down the insights). As you did for the first four days, speak the questions both silently and aloud and let the answers flow.

Notice how these questions shift the emphasis from *your will* and aspirations to *Spirit's Will* and aspirations for you. It involves a greater willingness to let Spirit work through you:

Write: Beloved Indwelling Spirit, what is Your Highest Aspiration for me—that which You would have me fulfill? What do You desire to accomplish through me?

As you meditate on these questions, you will be getting your little self out of the way and letting Spirit express Its true desires for you.

Do not be discouraged if the answers are vague or not immediately forthcoming. Remember, these questions are working at a deeper level beyond the intellect and the answers may come in a different form than you would expect. You may not necessarily receive full-blown answers, but instead only partial beginnings.

Be alert and aware of what is going on in your life, the people you meet, and casual remarks heard. Leadings come in unusual ways when you are working with Spirit.

As you receive insights, trust them. Do not let your fearful little ego throw up logical arguments or worldly reasons as to why you can't take the route shown by these higher insights. Have the courage to go for it and follow through, even though you are not entirely sure of how to proceed.

Ask your Inner Counselor the question:

Beloved Indwelling Spirit, what is the first action step You want me to take toward my goal, beginning today?

Again, get quiet, shift to your nondominant hand, and let this first step come forth. It may be a very small step. It may even seem a little vague, but step out on faith and take action in whatever way presents itself.

As you take this step today, it will sharpen your awareness of your purpose. It will give you a feeling of rightness that will be like the radio beam which guides the airline pilot safely to his destination.

After you have accomplished the first step, ask the same question again in meditation and receive the next action step. Do this meditative inquiry daily so that your Indwelling Guide can instruct you.

The ancient writer of Proverbs knew this process of checking in daily with our Guide when he wrote:

"In all thy ways acknowledge him, and he will direct thy paths" (Prov. 3:6 ASV).

Listening to your Intuitive Guide is the secret of finding your way, rather than listening to the voice of the intellect that only confuses you with doubt. Know that your Indwelling Spirit will be working through you and will be providing you with courage, love, and all the resources necessary to your success.

The entire universe will flow to fill the vessel of your earnest desire, just as the entire ocean flows to fill a hole dug by a small child with a tiny shovel by the edge of the sea. *You* are that beloved child.

Whenever I feel discouraged or feel I have lost my way, I reread the inspiring words of Emma Curtis Hopkins:

> Trust your hope. Never mind who tells you the particulars of downfall or disaster—trust your hope. It is a branch from the deathless soul that dwells in you as the true vine or true creation of God. . . .

Your highest aspiration is that which you are intended to fulfil, and if you have heretofore let any environments or circumstances sap your confidence in your aspirations, it is time you pruned your ideas. . . .

"I am the true vine. The way I begin to reign in you is when you trust your highest aspirations, your only hope, and prune boldly the tremblings of apprehension, of short-sightedness of prophecies of evil. Nothing shall prevail against Me," says Jesus Christ, in man the hope of glory.[3]

Chapter 5

Empowering
Your
Discovery

Using the insights you gained from the Seven Day Discovery Process, create a focused prayer statement describing your right work as you deem it to be. Don't outline *how* it will come about—that is God's work. Simply try to get it into focus.

Begin with a sentence thanking your Higher Power for placing you in this right work: "Thank You for—" Then continue by describing and defining the overall scope of the work as you understand it to be—a broad job description.

By giving thanks in advance, you are stating your trust in your Senior Partner. Your gratitude creates a magnet that attracts your desire to you. It also shapes and forms your desire—creating a mold into which the universal substance can pour itself.

End the description with this statement: "Let it be this or something better, according to Your wise and loving Will, not mine, for the highest good of all concerned."

This is a statement surrendering your desire to your Higher Power, saying in effect, "This is the way that I see it; however, I defer to Your wise and loving judgment for my highest good."

Test the Sincerity of Your Prayer

Now apply the eight tests of a sincere prayer, as given in the Bible—

"Whatsoever things are *true,*
whatsoever things are *honorable,*
whatsoever things are *just,*
whatsoever things are *pure,*
whatsoever things are *lovely,*
whatsoever things are of *good report;*
if there be any *virtue,* and if there be any *praise,*
think on these things."—Philippians 4:8 (ASV)

Application:

Whatsoever is true—practice daily visualizing your heart's desire *coming true* according to your Higher Power's goodwill for you. Know that in the invisible it is already true and is forming into visibility now.

Breathe in your prayer through your heart center.

Hold for a moment at the top of the breath and visualize your prayer *coming true.* As you exhale, silently speak, "Thank You."

Whatsoever is honorable—test your desire to see if it meets the standards of inner *honesty* and is fair to all concerned.

Whatsoever is just—feel yourself *justly* deserving and worthy of this desire coming true.

Whatsoever is pure—ask yourself if your desire is arising from a *pure* intention, not just a selfish ego motive.

Whatsoever is lovely— is it worth *loving?* Does it add to the goodness in the world?

Whatsoever is of good report—what would be a *good report* concerning your sincere desire? Visualize that good report coming to you. Feel the joy of receiving that good news. How would it feel to be in your right work? Get in touch with that feeling of fulfillment. Contemplate the joy of it.

When we pray rightly, we concentrate until we actually feel that desire fulfilled to the point where we can become it; we sense a collapsing of time and space until we actually are there. Feel the joy of being it, being there, having it.

This gives your prayer substance and reality in the spiritual plane. Then the holy marriage between your thinking and feeling nature takes place, and the offspring of that marriage—your desire—comes forth fulfilled. Then we have activated the law of reversibility, which states:

When you become one in consciousness with the fulfillment of your desire, then that in turn becomes the very cause which will bring about the desired effect.

Jesus taught this law when he said, "He that hath, to him shall be given" (Mk. 4:25 ASV). (The person who has the consciousness/the feeling of being one with the fulfillment of his or her desire shall receive.)

He emphasizes this oneness again, saying, "Whatsoever ye pray and ask for, believe that ye receive them, and ye shall have them" (Mk. 11:24 ASV). (Believe and feel as if you already have your desire in hand—make it virtual reality—and you shall have it.)

If there be any virtue—check to see if it meets the *highest standard* of the soul's sincere desire or the loving will of God.

If there is any praise—*praise* God and give thanks for the fulfillment of your desire in God's own way. Surrender it completely—"Thy loving, wonderful Will be done, not mine, for the highest good of all concerned."

Construct a Visual Prayer Chart

Visual prayer charts are a very effective way to pray, because they make use of the language of pictures and symbols that impact our mind more strongly than words alone. They engage the strongest of our inner powers—our imagination.

These charts are usually made on a large poster board on which you paste your definite prayer statement describing your new work, together with dramatic pictures, illustrations, and diagrams that symbolize success, fulfillment, prosperity, service, and so forth. (An alternate is a smaller blank-paged book that can be kept confidential.)

Old magazines, especially those of a positive or inspirational nature, are an excellent source for pictures, prayers, and headlines for your chart.

Note carefully what the picture and background depict. I knew a teacher who was dating a wonderful man and was praying that he would propose. She found a picture of two intertwined wedding rings nestled in a golden bird's nest. Her students began bringing in birds' nests to her at school!

Her boyfriend did propose. Later she showed him the prayer chart, and he was highly amused! They began making prayer charts for their marriage goals and have found them to be very helpful.

Inner Activity # 11   Visual Prayer Chart

Head your chart with a statement, picture, or symbol of the Divine Source from which all success and well-being flows.

Use positive I Am statements throughout to describe your desire. Example:

I Am a wise, capable leader.
I Am richly and abundantly prospered in my new work.
I Am filled with successful and prospering ideas.

Paste your pictures and affirmative statements in a flow-chart order, moving in sequence toward fulfillment.

Finish your chart with this final statement:

"Thank You, Holy Spirit. Let it be this or something better, according to Your wonderful, loving will for my life. I relax and trust the process. Amen."

This reaffirms your trust and lets you release any concern for results.

Pray your chart at night before going off to sleep. This places it in the "Crock-Pot" of your subconscious to "cook" all night. Read it again in the morning—knowing that Spirit will be working behind the scenes to arrange whatever It desires to accomplish through you. Release it and trust the process.

Using Your
Waiting Time Creatively

Chapter 6

Using Spiritual Skills for Conflict Resolution

While you are waiting for the door of your new opportunity to open, you can use your present work as a spiritual training ground. Every job, even an unhappy one, can provide you with an opportunity to hone your people skills and practice working with your Inner Partner.

Every day we are presented with situations that test our ability to see beyond apparent trouble and negativity—to the Higher Truth of the situation. These tests usually involve personality conflicts and disagreements with fellow workers, bosses, or customers.

We can try to solve these problems on the level of the

problem by using a variety of psychological conflict-resolution methods, but there won't be any permanent solution until we solve them on the higher spiritual level, as we did with the Freedom and Release Letter.

Then we will be acting from our spiritual center instead of from our defensive ego. Acting from our lower nature always compounds the problem!

I keep a sign on my desk that says, "Come Up Higher." It reminds me to see people and situations from a higher perspective. Our souls' highest assignments in this earth experience are to remember to love ourselves and others unconditionally.

We can't really do this until we know there is something worth loving in us in the first place. If all we ever see of ourselves and others is the outer personality, with its flaws and many faces of fear, anger, self-doubt, and defensiveness, we may never find anything to love, much less anything to resolve conflicts.

Here are four spiritual methods to help you work from your higher nature to solve conflicts in the workplace.

Figure #5   **Flip the Box**

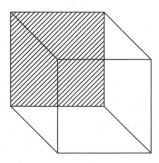

1. "Flip the box"

As you look into this diagram, you may see the box "open" at the top or perhaps at the side. There are two or three possible illusions contained in the drawing. Blink your eyes back and forth until your perspective suddenly shifts and you can see the box open in a new way. You have "flipped the box."

The diagram is like a situation in life—it contains both the problem and the solution within it. *Life will always deliver to us according to our attitudes and how we view it.*

Don't get locked into one way of seeing a situation. It may be that you are letting your negative attitudes "box" you into only one way of seeing it.

Ask: *"How would my fearless Higher Self see this situation? What is the good hidden here?"* As you ask these questions, your perception shifts from the problem to the higher perspective. You see the situation or the person in a new way. You then "flip the box."

2. Use Praise

Praise is one of the best methods to help us change the way we view a situation or others, that is, "flip the box."

In troublesome situations, silently praise the Higher Self in the person with whom you are having difficulty. Watch as the emotional energy fueling the situation shifts from negative to positive, from disagreement to harmony.

The atmosphere "lightens up," because praise magnifies the Light. It is the magnet that draws forth the good in any situation or person. Even thankless situations will yield a blessing when we "flip the box" through praise.

A purchasing agent was having difficulty with his employer, who was being unreasonable and critical. He began to silently praise the good in the person during the day, beaming the blessing, "I praise the goodness of God in you."

In about a week's time, he noticed a decided improvement in their relations. He began to see his employer in a new way and to appreciate the better qualities in him. Soon they were working side by side in harmony.

Silently praise the goodness of God in your boss and your fellow workers every day. Beam the thought to them—*"I praise the goodness of God in you"* or *"I praise the good in you"* or *"Thank You, God, that You are at work here."* If there is anything in their performance that you can sincerely compliment or praise aloud, do so.

Watch and feel the energy at your workplace improve. As you approach your present work with this praiseful attitude, you will suddenly see some aspects of it you have not seen before—blessings that you would have missed had you continued in a resentful attitude.

A woman executive in one of my workshops related that before coming to her present position she had been with a large company on the West Coast. When she knew she was going to be leaving that position, she chose to adopt a positive attitude toward the remaining time there, instead of being negative or impatient.

Every day as she drove to work she repeated to herself, *"I will serve this company to the best of my ability today."*

She said that instead of getting restless, she was able to help other people on the job, and the transition time was wonderful. She had learned to "flip the box."

In another case, a wife was at her wit's end dealing with her very critical and irresponsible husband. He was often out of work and would spend his day drinking beer with the wrong crowd. While she couldn't find anything about him to praise in his present behavior, she fortunately realized that she could praise his higher nature beyond his faults and weaknesses.

She silently began praising that Higher Self of him and beaming the blessing, "I praise the goodness of God in you." Gradually she noticed a decided improvement in him as his better nature began to respond and express itself in positive ways. He found work and began to relate to her in a more loving and appreciative way.

Remember, you are a Light-bearer and your highest purpose is to bring Light and Love to your world. If we are going to let our Light shine, we must first clean the windows of our souls and dissolve the fears and negative attitudes that prevent the Light from shining through.

These spiritual methods are the Windex that will help with our cleaning. We can no longer say, "I don't do windows!"

3. "Behold the Christ"

One of the strongest methods for bringing the power of Light and Love into a workplace situation involves the use of the famous prayer poem "I Behold the Christ in You" by Frank B. Whitney.

This prayer is based on the Truth that at the core of our being, beyond the outer appearances and the changing personality of each one of us, is the Spirit of God that created us—the Source of Light, Love, and Wisdom in us. Whitney calls this extension of God into our nature "the Christ." Here is the prayer:

I behold the Christ in you,
    Here the life of God I see;
I can see a great peace too,
    I can see you whole and free.

I behold the Christ in you,
    I can see this as you walk;
I see this in all you do,
    I can see this as you talk.

I behold God's love expressed,
    I can see you filled with power;

I can see you ever blessed,
    See Christ in you hour by hour.

I behold the Christ in you,
    I can see that perfect one;
Led by God in all you do,
    I can see God's work is done.[1]

This is more than a beautiful prayer put to verse. As you study it, you will see that it touches on all levels of our lives—health, peace of mind, freedom, strength, and work. It is a powerful way to pray for someone.

When we call forth this Inner Presence in ourselves and others, it lifts us above the personality conflicts and the clash of egos. If you are in a confrontive situation with someone who is angry or upset, silently beam the thought *"I behold the Christ in you"* while looking the person in the eyes. You may find it more comfortable to look at the space between and slightly above their eyes.

This silent prayer message immediately lifts you out of your negative reactions. In seconds, both of you will calm down and harmony will be restored. Over the years, I have been continually astonished at how well this prayer works. It is truly amazing!

In my own experience, I have found that the most effective way to use the prayer is to write it out for the person involved in a quiet time alone. There is a kinesthetic connection between the hand and the heart that makes the praying more powerful.

I have used it in business situations to defuse explosive conflicts, as well as in personal relationships, and it always brings results. I usually write it out completely five times. Often I write it for myself first to calm down and shift out of my ego's negativity. You will find it much easier to write the prayer for another person, after you clear yourself spiritually of whatever is troubling you.

As you write it for yourself, you may experience a transition occurring. The first two times through, you are probably just copying the prayer, changing it from "you" to "myself"—"*I behold the Christ in myself,*" and so on. But by the third or fourth time—if you are writing with your left/nondominant hand—you may find the verses changing and your Higher Self now writing to you, speaking to your need and blessing you in specific ways.

Here is an example of how the prayer may come through:

I am the Christ in you that loves you.
I am the perfect life of God in you;
I am the great peace you seek,
I am that in you which is whole and free.
I am the Christ in you.
I go with you as you walk;
I am with you in all you do,
I am the Word expressing Itself as you talk.

I am God's love expressing Itself in you.
I fill you with spiritual power,
I am ever blessing you,
Moment by moment, hour by hour.

I am the Christ in you.
I am that perfect one;
I lead you in all that you do,
I see that God's work is done.

Immediately you feel recentered and reconnected with that loving Source of your being. Now seeing beyond the appearances, you can more easily write the prayer for the other person involved.

As you begin to write, you will find yourself breaking out of the rote copying, as additional lines and insights flow off the end of your pen. You are gaining the "Ah-ha" with the deeper insights into the other person and the origins of your inharmony. You are tapping into the higher levels of understanding, where the true solutions await you. The prayer will turn out to be filled with extra lines of blessing.

I have never seen this prayer method fail. It always brings harmony and understanding, because the real work is being done on the higher spiritual levels of consciousness. Not you, but the "Christ" within you is doing the work.

The greatest change will be felt in yourself. You will feel lighter, calmer, and more centered. The outer inharmonies will soon yield to this spiritual power. To bring a deeper breakthrough for longstanding issues involving family members, I have seen individuals write out the basic prayer five times daily for seven days. It is a wonderful prayer to use for troubled or ill children. Children are especially sensitive to the vibrations around them and they respond to the prayer marvelously. Parents can also speak it softly to sleeping children. When they awaken, they will be much improved.

One of our workshop participants received a very angry phone call at work. She happened to have the prayer by the phone and began praying it silently for the person. In a few minutes the invisible prayer took effect, and the conversation finished on a positive note.

Another one of our participants tried the experiment of speaking the prayer to herself as she stood in front of a mirror. She said it was a dramatic and powerful experience!

A nurse working with psychiatric patients told me of how she uses a variation of this method in an effective way. She envisions the face of Jesus overlaid on her patients' faces as she ministers to them. She notices a decided improvement in their behavior.

4. Use this inner question: "Who's doing this?"

This simple question will remind you to turn any task over to your Higher Power to accomplish through you. "Who's doing this?" will trigger the answer, "God is doing this," or "I Am"—the name of God within you. Your attention is immediately shifted to your Higher Power, and you can call upon It to help you with the task. The results will be much better than anything you could do on your own.

Try this method with special business projects that

you are not sure how to handle. "Who is making this business deal?" "Who is making this sales call?" "Who is preparing this bid?" Immediately you connect with the wisdom of your Inner Partner, and the work is done much better than if you had continued on your own.

Try it while driving home from work in rush-hour traffic when you are usually tired and stressed out. "Who's driving?" "God is." "I Am." You'll find yourself relaxing and driving more safely, with a lot less stress. You also may hear Spirit answer your question with a little joke about your poor driving habits!

Carrying on a dialogue with your Inner Partner will keep your mind centered, instead of drifting off into negative scenarios.

A friend of mine, a former military officer, practices this idea in his daily work. Instead of making a long list of "things that have to be done today," he starts the day by reporting to "Headquarters."

He told me, with a smile, "I begin my day with this prayer: 'Reporting for duty, Sir. I await your orders.' Then I sit quietly for a time and follow through on whatever silent instructions I receive about the business at hand. My day usually flows easily and in good order."

One of my favorite prayers is one that I first used in business whenever I was feeling uptight about a problem with deliveries, suppliers, or deadlines.

POCKET PRAYER POWER

There is only One Power and One Presence in my
life and in the Universe—
God, the Good, Omnipotent.
Right now, this very moment, this very hour,
God is setting things right and arranging my affairs
for my Highest Good, and I am grateful.

Praying this prayer always shifted me from trying to solve the problem on my own to calling on my Partner's help. Invariably the outer problem would resolve itself, sometimes in a very unusual way. I kept the prayer on a card in my pocket until I eventually memorized it and could call it to mind at will. You may wish to copy it and laminate it for your own use.

Chapter 7

Overcoming
the
Dragons
of
Discouragement

D uring your time of waiting for your right work, you may find your little, fearful ego indulging in its favorite habit of gnawing on some old "worry bone" it has dug up from the backyard of the subconscious.

The ego fears the unknown and cannot see how everything will work out. The *"what ifs?"* begin to surface—"What if I leave the security of my old job, and I don't make a go of my new career? What if I make a new beginning and fail? What if I can't pay the mortgage?"

These nagging fears drain our energy field faster than any physical exertion. The more energy we invest in these worries, the bigger they get and the greater the drain on our energy. Eventually we experience a "brownout" like New York City suffers in the middle of a prolonged heat wave when the extra electrical demand of air conditioners exceeds the power plant's capacity. Our brownouts are nervous exhaustion and the inability to make decisions.

Detach From the Trash

The first step in overcoming these nagging worries is to <u>stand back and observe them</u>. As soon as you switch from feeling like a victim to being a dispassionate observer, you can take control of these fears.

Become the observer by mentally stepping outside yourself and asking, "Who's worrying here?" The answer will probably be "Me" or "I am." Then ask, "Who has the power to dispel this worry?" The answer to this last question will shift your attention from the problem to your Higher Power, the Source of all answers—the Mind That Knows within you. As soon as you make this shift, the emotional-energy drain stops.

In another analogy, think of each fear thought as an infant dragon that feeds on our negative emotional energy. The more we fear and worry, the more we feed the little dragon and the bigger and stronger it grows, until it scares the living faith out of us!

As soon as we stop fretting about the problem and shift our attention to the Power and Presence of God, the dragons will die of starvation.

Of all the dragons we face, none is more deadly to our success than the dragon of discouragement. Nothing will erode our confidence more quickly than discouragement. If you have ever awakened in the middle of the night with a dragon of discouragement sitting heavily on your chest so that you can hardly breathe, you know how frightening it can be!

On one such night I learned a valuable lesson about handling discouragement. I was involved in a building project and had taken too much of the responsibility for its success upon my own shoulders. I forgot to shift the burden to my Senior Partner. I awoke in the middle of the night, with the "dragon" sitting on my chest, fiery eyes glaring, roaring at me for attention!

Somehow, I was prompted to dialogue with this oppressive feeling of discouragement, so I took a pad and pencil from the bedside table and addressed it, as follows:

I asked: "Discouragement, what is your purpose? Why are you hanging over me?"

To my amazement the answer came:

"My Lord, you need me! Without me, you would not rise up with courage and faith. I exercise your faith muscles. I am your trainer. I exercise you for victory!"

Astounded, I replied, "Bless you and thank you, thou good and faithful servant!"

What a tremendous insight! I felt immediately relieved. My faith and courage were being strengthened through this strenuous course of discouragement. It was my trainer, much as the unorthodox trainer in the classic movie *Chariots of*

Fire developed the running strength of the Olympic track star.

Notice how Discouragement addressed me as "My Lord," signifying that I was its master. Notice how I called it, "thou good and faithful servant."

This very discouragement with which I was struggling was actually building my faith muscles to help me meet my challenge. Because of it I was forced to find the inner fortitude I would not have developed if things had been easy.

More important, it brought me to the *point of surrender*—to the point where I was ready to stop trying to do it all myself and turn the project over to my Senior Partner. As soon as I shifted the burden, conditions improved on the building project.

It taught me the all-important lesson that only by returning in conscious awareness to the One Power and Intelligence can we find the solution to our difficulties.

Dialogue With Whatever Is Troubling You

Dialoguing will help you objectify the trouble—get it out in the open, where you can look at it. Then you can extract the message it has for you.

Simply take a quiet time with pen and notebook to address whatever is troubling you. You may already have an idea of what this is, but you need to zero in on the root of the heavy feeling. If this is the case, simply address the dark feeling. For example:

"Dark Feeling, who are you? What are you connected with? Identify yourself."

Sit quietly and let the intuitive answers come through, as you write with your nondominant hand.

Continue your dialogue as you feel led, possibly asking, "What is your purpose? What message are you bringing me that I need to know—that will help me?"

Carry through until you feel at peace, which signifies you have received the blessing. Always end with an expression of gratitude for the insight that has been given to you.

Observe Your Dreams

Your Indwelling Spirit may also use dreams to get through to you. Dreams can be rich resources of valuable answers when your intuition may be blocked with worry.

When you have a vivid dream, capture it. Write it down immediately, before it slips away from you upon fully awakening. Describe it in detail and be sure to describe the feelings you had in the dream. Then dialogue with its major characters, objects, and events. Ask of each one, "What do you represent in me, and what message do you have for me?" You will get surprising answers, especially if you write the answers with your nondominant hand to access your right brain.

Here is a dream I had on another restless night when I went to bed distraught, in the face of many challenges in my life at the time:

I was struggling along a dark passageway, trying to reach a doorway of deliverance that had light streaming through it. But the door was guarded by two ferocious dragon-like creatures that roared at me horribly. They frightened me so badly that I became angry and roared back at them as loud as I could!

To my utter amazement, they rolled over on their backs, cringing and whimpering like two scared puppies, and began to lick my hands. At that, I laughed out loud as I watched their antics. I petted and comforted them, and they began to play and frolic around my feet. Together we walked through the door of deliverance into the light beyond.

When I awoke, I was completely free of my fear and discouragement. I intuitively knew these horrible creatures, symbolizing my terrible problems, were nothing to fear.

They only wanted my love and attention. I was their master and, like animals, they had sensed my fears and were reflecting them back to me. They were as frightened as I was, and their angry roaring was only an expression of their fear. They really only wanted to be loved. *Our problems are our own fears reflected back to us, waiting for our love, reassurance, and attention.*

All of the power and energy I had expended to empower the problems, I was able to reclaim and use to recharge myself. I was reintegrated, whole, and free. I was now able to view the problems in my life with a positive new perspective. I turned them over to my Senior Partner to handle, and they soon were resolved in a wonderful way.

Notice the importance of laughter in the dream. Humor and laughter will dispel discouragement faster than any other remedy. It is a great healer of mind and body. To be able to laugh at ourselves, our fears, and foibles immediately re-empowers us and changes our energy from negative to positive.

Practice laughing at yourself in the mirror every morning when you first get up—grumpy, sleepy, hair uncombed. Make a few faces at yourself, flash a big smile, and say, "You're looking terrific this morning! You're going to make it! God is in charge!"

Stop Fretting and Start Letting

If you examine your life, you will see how you have been led by devious ways through many detours, to the place where you are now. Nothing happens by chance. The detours were necessary because you were so busy fretting that you would not follow the way Spirit intended you to go—the straight and the short route. So you were led around the obstacles that you created for yourself.

In your daily quiet time, remind yourself of the following Truth:

God has a plan for my life.
I do not have to know everything in advance.
I only need to keep moving ahead
one step at a time, knowing
that the way is being made clear.
My Higher Power is working through me
to accomplish whatever is for my highest good.
I relax in this knowing.
I keep my eyes open for opportunities to serve.
I keep my ears open for guidance.
I stop fretting and start letting God be in charge.
I listen, obey, and enjoy!

Finally, remember that you are part of Something Greater. Although you may have forgotten this and feel you are all alone struggling through life, the Truth is that you are actually the point man for a much larger Power. You are the person on the playing field at this time. You are backed up by an invisible Circle of Support that is beyond your knowing and is waiting to be recognized and called upon.

As Jesus had his twelve legions of angels, so you have your own Band of Support—a heavenly host all working on your behalf. You can call upon this loving Power by declaring in the midst of your discouragement—*"I am a part of Something Greater that loves and provides for me. I take heart and know that with the help of my Higher Power, I will triumph over every obstacle in my pathway."*

Step out and take a bold action to restore your confidence and get back in step with your Higher Power. Begin to use this spiritual formula: *Faith + Obedience to the Higher Will = the Confidence to Command.*

As you begin to exercise your faith in line with the Higher Will, you receive the confidence to command this Power from within.

In other words, Spirit says, "If you will put your trust in Me and obey My higher guidance, I will give you the power to command Me." The two great Hebrew prophets Isaiah and Jeremiah spoke of this: "Thus says the Lord . . . concerning the work of My hands, you command Me." (Is. 45:11 NKJV) and "Behold, I *am* the Lord, . . . Is there anything too hard for Me?" (Jer. 32:27 NKJV)

Chapter 8

Sorting Out Ego Delays From <mark>Divine</mark> Delays

E ven though we hold to our faith that our Higher Power is working behind the scenes arranging our right new work, we are often plagued with a sense of delay and a feeling that things are not going right.

Perhaps you are feeling like the woman who applied for admission to a training school for a new career. She had excellent qualifications for acceptance but was turned down and told to reapply in one year. She was terribly disappointed and could not understand what went wrong.

She carried the situation into meditation and received the insight that "God's delays are not God's denials." She realized that she had some emotional situations in her personal life which needed resolving before she could enter the school with a free mind. She came to the understanding that the postponement was really a "divine delay" and began to appreciate the wisdom of it.

Reasons for Delay

If you are experiencing delay now, consider the following possibilities:

1. Your goal is Spirit-directed, and you are on the right track, but you are not really ready yet.

You still have some major blocks that haven't been cleared. Now is the time to bite the bullet and face those that you have been avoiding. Review the methods outlined in Chapter 2 to help you clear those blocks.

2. Your goal is Spirit-directed and you are ready, but the timing is not yet right. You are in a holding pattern.

Like an aircraft circling an airport, you are waiting for the control tower to give you clearance. People and events have to be brought into the right alignment and sequence before you can move forward.

The woman who had experienced the "divine delay" also intuited that there were possibly people who would be important to her who would not be intersecting her path at school until the following year.

In another analogy, it is like those little puzzles that are made up of a series of sliding tiles with one space empty. The idea is to slide the tiles around one by one until they can be positioned to spell a word or create a picture.

So, too, all things in your life must be shifted around until all is just right—until it spells "go forward" for you. Stay open—easy for Spirit to "slide," so you will be able to move quickly when the window of opportunity opens.

3. Your fearful ego is the holdup.

Your codependent ego doesn't want to let go of the "security blankets" of the old job and old relationships or the comfort zone of familiar surroundings. Your ship of opportunity sails on the outgoing tide. Make up your mind and leap on board. You can't keep one foot on the dock and one foot on the ship. You will do a split and fall into the water!

4. You may have locked on to the wrong goal.

It is ego-driven instead of Spirit-directed. You may be following a strong ego desire that has eclipsed your original leadings from Spirit. You have unwittingly sidetracked yourself. Your Senior Partner is waiting patiently to redirect you onto your right course. Check your motives. Ask yourself, "Why am I really applying for this position or pursuing this course of action?" See whether your reasons are really constructive and in alignment with your Higher Purpose.

Look back to your Seven-Day Discovery Process in Chapter 4. Compare the answers gained there with the path you are now trying to pursue. See if they are tracking together.

Positive Actions

Here are some positive actions you can take while you are waiting:

1. Make a beginning.

Remember, your Inner Partner cannot give you any guidance while you are biting your nails in a state of indecision as to which road to take. Have the courage to step out in some direction, and then Spirit will either open the way or give you a course correction—telling you to make a ninety-degree turn to the right or left or even giving you a stop sign!

Simply take a few small steps in that direction, and you will feel the inner guidance that says, "Yes, that feels natural and right." If on the other hand, you feel a sense of pressure about it, a resistance or a sense of dark negativity about it—stop. Let go of it.

A young man wistfully wished he could leave his dishwashing job and go to college to study library science, but he couldn't afford it. He felt stuck.

I said to him: "Your first step toward your goal won't cost you any money. Go to the local community college and pick up their catalog of courses. Select the courses you want to take, and then put your prayer power to work. The way will open for you, but not until you stop wishing and start moving your feet."

As the saying goes, "If you want to win the lottery, you've got to buy a ticket!" Sitting home wishing and praying to God won't help you win. You've got to put yourself into the flow!

2. Learn in advance everything you can about your prospective field of choice.

In the process of saturating yourself with information about your field of choice, you will also get a confirmation of whether or not this field is really right for you.

"Shirley" was a housewife who had attended one of my self-improvement classes. She decided she wanted to be a travel agent. She thought: "Oh, wouldn't it be wonderful! I could travel to the Egyptian pyramids and guide trips through Europe!"

It all sounded so romantic, but when she began to study the work, she found that 90 percent of the time she would have her nose glued to a computer screen tediously looking up airline fares and flight schedules, and she would be on the phone incessantly.

Yes, there would be occasional trips to the pyramids, but gone were her romantic, uninformed notions. She saw much more realistic aspects of the travel business that she needed to weigh and consider.

With her eyes wide open, she finally made the decision and is now a fine travel agent. The more you study your field of choice, the more you will be able to see whether or not it is really right for you.

If you are going to have an interview with a particular employer, find out everything you possibly can about that company before the interview—study its history, its product line, its markets. The interviewer will be pleased that you have done your homework and that you are really interested in the company and its goals and not just in what the company can do for you.

3. Get in the flow by volunteering in your field of choice.

Put the law of giving and receiving to work for you. Find a way to volunteer in your field of choice. You will be helping and giving of yourself at the same time you are learning the work. You will be placing yourself in a position to take advantage of the window of opportunity when it opens. You will have the inside hiring track.

I told the young man who was interested in becoming a librarian, "Go to the head librarian at the college and ask if there is some volunteer work you can do to help you get acquainted with your field of interest."

Mark Twain, I recall, used this method successfully when he was a young man seeking work on the western frontier. Jobs were hard to find, but Twain went to a construction site and told the boss that he would work for one week free to show the quality of his work. The boss was delighted, and sure enough, at the end of the week, he gave Twain a job. Mark Twain put the law of giving and receiving to work, and it paid off for him. You have to give in order to receive. What are you willing to give?

4. Be patient.

The goals we have been praying for will be worked out in God's own way and time, not ours. Becoming impatient only saps our positive attitude and leads to discouragement. We humans want action, and we want it right away, so we are often tempted to jump at something too soon. Having to sit back and trust that Spirit is at work behind the scenes can be difficult, especially when we can't see the path ahead.

Doubts creep in and erode our confidence.

Think of bodysurfing in the ocean and waiting to catch the right wave. It means waiting, watching the small waves go by, watching for the big one—seeing it swell and curl, and then leaping in front of it just before it crests! In our career change we must wait and trust, watch "the sea of opportunity" swell, and leap when the wave crests!

This means staying tuned in to your Inner Counselor in your daily quiet time. This will keep you tuned to the right frequency so that when Spirit gives you a signal or sends a serendipitous opportunity your way, you will recognize it and be able to act on it.

Remember, *"God's delays are not God's denials."*

Chapter 9

Exchanging Financial Worry for True Security

D uring our time of waiting we often feel the dragon of financial worry breathing down our neck. We see bills piling up and our bank account dwindling. It becomes so easy to forget the Truth that God is our unfailing supply.

But just as finding our right work is an *inside job*, so finding our true financial security is also an *inside job*. It must come from an inner consciousness of All-sufficiency. There is no need to spend our lives grubbing for a living in the midst of God's grandeur, when all the while the Intelligence that created us is waiting to sustain us so It can work Its purposes through us.

E. V. Ingraham expresses this idea from an enlightened perspective in his book *Wells of Abundance:*

The same Power that produced Heaven and earth must necessarily sustain them. The Power that created must be the Life and Substance of the created. That Power moved to create and now must move to sustain. These facts must stand as the eternal law of being, Therefore,

My supply of all good is at hand. The Wealth of Heaven and earth move toward me on the current of Infinite creative Power. The tide of God's creative Power, the Spirit of God that moved to create, still moves. It moves to sustain me and all creation. It moves with pleasure to express and fulfill itself in me here and now. With eagerness, it floods my whole being, pressing itself out into complete expression through my mind and flesh and into my affairs.

I inherit the Wealth of the Universe and it eagerly and actively seeks me out, pouring its great Wealth upon me. The Riches of the Kingdom flood my whole being.

I am richly and abundantly supplied within and without from the eager storehouse of the Universe, a supply that is more eager to manifest Wealth through me than I am eager to receive it. I open my whole being wide that the eager abundance of God may enrich me and all of my world.[1]

The pure logic of this statement is stunning! It blows away the dark cloud of worry that hangs over us, and something deep within us resonates with this truth.

We are here to serve as instruments through which Spirit can work, and therefore it is in Spirit's highest interests to provide for us. Know then that the Power that created you will not and *cannot* fail you. Any failure is on our parts, because we fail to honor our Partnership.

Our job as junior partners is to keep our inner eye on our Partner and do the legwork. It is our Partner's responsibility to guide us and supply all the resources necessary to success. Our minds are the connecting links with this Source, and by keeping our attention focused on this Source, instead of on the financial appearances, we will open the flow of supply as needed.

The Divine "Waiting Adequate"

Emma Curtis Hopkins calls this Source the *"Waiting Adequate."* What a wonderful description! Whenever you are feeling bullied by the dragon of financial worry, lift your inner vision to the divine *Waiting Adequate*. The ancient teachings of the Upanishads tell us, "I have given thee an eye divine with which to behold My power." [2]

It is this "eye divine" that we must lift above the worrisome appearances. "It is the lifting up of this sense out of the network of materiality, the wheel of incessant grind, that takes man above his disasters and difficulties."[3]

The Master, Jesus, showed us how to do this when he was faced with the impossible task of feeding the crowds of people who had come to hear him speak. He shifted his attention from that need to the Power which could fill any need and more—the divine Waiting Adequate.

In the face of impossible appearances he "looked up" to his All-Providing Father and gave thanks in advance, thereby showing his complete trust in the Source to provide under every circumstance. He then proceeded to divide and distribute what was at hand. The divine Waiting Adequate fed the entire crowd, with plenty to spare!

A good affirmation for you to use is: *Through the power of the divine Waiting Adequate, I have plenty to share and plenty to spare, and I am grateful!*

So when you are faced with the bills piling up and what appears to be a "no-way" situation, follow the Master's three steps: (1) Take your mind off the need (which has no power of itself to ever produce supply) and "look up" to the Source and "see" the divine supply flowing to you, (2) Give thanks in advance, and (3) Step out on faith and fearlessly distribute whatever you have at hand. Let the divine Waiting Adequate take care of multiplying the resources. You will be surprised at how your resources begin to stretch.

This is the higher way of the Partnership—looking to our Senior Partner for supply. This is the way of the twenty-first century, which goes beyond the stressful methods of producing prosperity by mental effort and affirmation, to the higher, spiritual way of knowing our oneness with the Source. This is the difference between the lower way of "taking the Kingdom by force" (of will and mental manipulation) to the calm knowing that "all that the Father has is mine."

Tithing

One of the most powerful ways of establishing and maintaining your connection with the Source is to make an "investment in faith."

The ancient writers of the Bible understood this spiritual principle that the more we invest in our faith in God as the unfailing Source of our supply, the stronger our faith becomes. Our faith, in turn, controls the flow of God's good into our life. This investment principle was called tithing, that is, returning or reinvesting a tenth.

The prophet Malachi was aware of this investment principle when he wrote, "Bring ye all the tithes into the storehouse, that there may be meat in mine house, and prove me now herewith, saith the Lord of hosts, if I will not open you the windows of heaven, and pour you out a blessing, that there shall not be room enough to receive it" (Mal. 3:10 KJV).

Reinvest a portion of the resources channeled to you from the Source to wherever you are receiving your spiritual nourishment—to the organizations engaged in spiritual work. It may be a prayer ministry, a church, a spiritual meditation center, or from wherever or whomever you receive spiritual support and inspiration for your daily life.

Every time you are engaged in paying your weekly or monthly bills, write the first check to one of these organizations as a way of being grateful to Spirit for all that has been given to you—not only for finances, but also for health, love, and life itself!

This reaffirms your faith in Divine Adequacy to provide for you. It takes your eye off any appearance of lack, places it on the Source, and opens the flow of supply for you to redistribute as necessary.

With the writing of each tithe check, you are strengthening your faith and confidence that all of your needs will be met in the right way at the right time. You will be surprised at how this establishes order in your finances and increases your income, as well as contributes to your general well-being in all aspects of your life.

Living by the tithing principle activates the law of first priority, which states that *when we acknowledge God as first priority in our lives, all things flow in divine order to meet our requirements.* In my personal life I have found that this principle works without fail. The greater the portion you return to the Source in full faith and trust, the greater the blessings that flow into your life.

If you are fearful of beginning with the full tithe, start with a percentage with which you can feel comfortable. You may want to begin with 5 percent of your income until your faith and confidence in God builds so that you can return the full tithe, the full 10 percent. Do it regularly, without fail. Then you can experience the true inner security and dividends that come from cooperating with the law of first priority.

Tithing would seem to fly in the face of worldly reasoning that says, "The more you give, the less you have." In the material world, expenses deplete supply. But it is also a fact of the material world that *money invested earns returns*.

Tithing, rather than being an expense which depletes your bank account, is an *investment in the bank of God which always earns great returns*. When we provide investment capital for God's work, we are buying ownership in an invisible spiritual corporation that pays marvelous dividends, not only financially, but in terms of peace of mind, health, harmony, and happiness.

The practice of tithing also involves us in the law of circulation, so that the wellsprings of God's good are not blocked by our fear or selfishness, which can shut off the flow. Participation in God's Universal Mutual Support System requires circulation, giving, and receiving.

In the act of tithing we not only become aware of the presence of the Divine Giver and the Gift, we become, for that moment, the Giver and the Gift, in that we become the opening in the universe for the goodness of God to pour forth. Tithing thus becomes a sacred act, and we should always regard it as such. In this sacred act we are transformed from the limited human into the Divine Wellspring pouring forth a blessing for the world.

Riverbanks are always green. People who are tithers know that the more they open themselves to be channels for the flow of God's good, the more blessed their lives become. Just as riverbanks are always green, nourished by the precious water that they channel, so as you agree to become a channel for Spirit to work through, your life will become green and prosperous. The "green stuff" will flow!

Because of these benefits I have never known an ex-tither. Once people experience the benefits, true security, and peace of mind that come from tithing, they never go back to the old way of depending on the world to supply them. Tithing becomes their best investment.

One of my favorite prayers that envisions this flow of Divine Substance came to me during a time of great financial crisis.

Here it is for your use:

POCKET PRAYER POWER

All of God's channels for good are open
and flowing to me now.
Down from the high mountain of Spirit,
and across the broad plains of abundant substance—
my good flows to me from every direction,
from far away and near,
through people I've never before heard of
and people very dear,
And best of all from my Christ kingdom within.
Gratefully I share it to bless others.

It helps me to know that the flow is already on its way, through the right channels, and I simply have to "look up" to the "high mountain of Spirit," give thanks, and act in faith.

Our Consciousness Magnet

So we find that true prosperity is an *inside* job. It is not a rich bank account. It is the rich consciousness *behind* the bank account. It is the consciousness that creates and fills the bank account. We need to ask ourselves, "What is my consciousness attracting—lack or abundance?" It is a magnet that draws to us accordingly.

Our *consciousness magnet* attracts to us according to its strength—the strength of our belief in lack or the strength of our belief in God as our permanent Source of supply. "The rich get richer and the poor get poorer," according to their consciousness. As above in consciousness, so below in the material world. Build first a consciousness of God as unfailing supply, and all things will be added unto you.

Jesus taught this principle when he said, "For whosoever hath, to him shall be given, and he shall have abundance" (Mt. 13:12 ASV). To those who have a rich consciousness of God as supply, more will be given.

Inventor and electronic engineer, Bill Lear was a man with a rich consciousness. He tapped into the flow of prospering ideas springing from the Source and acted upon them. From that flow sprang more than 150 patents, including the first car radio. Later he pioneered the age of the business and private jet with the development of his Lear Jet.

Bill Lear was a man of many business ventures, and like most inventors, he had his failures as well as his successes. His bank accounts fluctuated up and down many times.

The story is told that someone once asked him, "Bill, don't you ever worry about going bankrupt with all these schemes of yours?" Bill is said to have replied, "No, because they can't bankrupt my mind." His prosperity consciousness apparently was always intact.

Jesus of Nazareth never had a bank account. As a matter of fact, he possessed almost nothing. But it is recorded that he did own one thing of great value—a beautiful and costly seamless robe. It was so desirable that the soldiers at the foot of the cross cast dice to possess it.

The movie *The Robe,* based on the Lloyd C. Douglas novel, tells the story of how the robe of Jesus went from hand to hand and transformed the lives of all those who touched it. It transformed them because it was imbued with the consciousness of the Master.

The Master's seamless robe symbolizes his magnificent consciousness—without seam or tear, without doubt or limitation of God's power to always provide for him. He "owned" the idea of his oneness with the Source of All-sufficiency, as expressed in his words, "All that the Father has is mine" and "I and the Father are one."

With such a powerful awareness, he didn't need a bank account, for whatever he required in the moment he could manifest, because he was one with its Source.

So what we need to ask ourselves is, *"What do I really own?"* Like a magnet, we can only own what our consciousness is capable of attracting and holding. It holds us at a certain level of affluence, or poverty, as the case may be.

"Own" the belief that you deserve the best, and you will draw the best to you. "Own" the idea that "all that the Father has is mine" to use and to share, and you will receive it.

Discard your threadbare consciousness—the tattered old beggar's robe riddled with holes of lack and worry, and put on the robe of God's All-sufficiency.

At the start of every day you have a choice. Which will you wear—the tattered one, or the Master's seamless robe? Make a conscious choice immediately, for it will clothe you for the rest of the day. Contemplate this image in the following meditation.

Meditation

Close your eyes, relax your tense muscles, and take a few slow, deep breaths. Imagine yourself in your bed. It is morning, and you are just awakening to the new day. Sleepily you swing your legs out of bed and, out of habit, reach for your old robe lying there.

Suddenly you see the Master in his seamless robe standing by your bed, radiant in the morning sunlight. He holds out the rich and elegant seamless robe to you.

He says to you, "Here is my robe of God's All-sufficiency. Will you take it and wear it with my blessing?"

With great joy and gratitude, you stand and feel his strong hands place it on your shoulders. You slip your arms through and wrap it around you. You feel its warmth, comfort, and security.

You hear yourself saying, "This is the day the Lord has made. I will put on the seamless robe and rejoice!"

Chapter 10

Looking Inward Before Successful Interviews

W hether you have been guided to work on your own or you will be working for someone else, the art of successful interviews is vital. Many of the same points apply to meeting with customers and clients, suppliers and creditors, as well as employers.

There are many books dealing with the outer factors of successful interviews. But beyond these are some very important *inner factors*.

1. What is your motive?

The interviewer primarily wants to know if you and he or she have the same interest—that is, what *you* can do for *the company*. This is your main point of agreement.

Too many people go into an interview wanting to hear what the *company* can do for them—salary, benefits, and so forth. If the interviewer is convinced that you are truly interested in the company's welfare and have something to offer, he or she will bring up the salary and benefits issues accordingly.

This principle of motive applies to your clients and suppliers as well—they want to know whether you are sincerely interested in them and have their interests at heart. They intuitively sense whether or not you are sincere.

2. Find agreement

Ask yourself, "Am I in agreement with the company's products and services?"—that is, is the company producing or offering a product or service which is beneficial to society, one which you can believe in morally, ethically, and environmentally?

You want to go to work every morning happy to know that you are contributing in some way to the common good of humanity, and not working in a weapons factory!

I once counseled a man who actually was working in an ammunition factory in the Midwest. He spent every day on the production line making .50-caliber machine-gun shells. Even though he was building up a nice pension, he knew he had to quit making bullets, which would kill and maim fellow human beings.

He finally left to take a lower-paying job doing something that would give him peace of mind. He eventually worked his way up to a good position with that company.

In connection with finding agreement, check out the "vibes." The prospective workplace has some important information for you. As you enter the grounds and building, pay attention to the gut-level feelings you receive.

What is the spirit of the place? Does it have a light feeling, or does it have a heavy, negative atmosphere? Does it feel like a harmonious place to work? Do the employees you pass or meet seem pleasant? Can you put your heart into working there?

These feelings are more important than any statistical analysis you may have made of the company and its prospects. Spreadsheets do not reveal these hidden factors.

3. Do your prayer work before leaving home

Remind yourself that you are going into the interview with the idea that since God is in charge, it will either be this position or something better, for the highest good of all concerned according to God's wonderful will. This takes the major pressure off you. It is not a do-or-die situation. You can be your natural, interested self.

You can go in knowing that if this is your right work, it will open for you. You can relax, breathe out any anxiety, and go with the flow of Spirit.

Here is a simple prayer to keep your mind positive and let God be in charge:

POCKET PRAYER POWER

The Spirit of the Lord goes before me
and conducts this meeting
for the highest good of all concerned.
Only good can come to me.

---

4. Center yourself before the actual interview

As you go into the interview, take a moment to balance your energy field so that you are relaxed and poised before the interview.

Slowly breathe in on "Peace," and out on "Be Still." Smile. Lighten up! Use your inner vision to send a blessing of light and harmony into the room ahead of you. Silently pray, *The Spirit of the Lord is in charge of this interview, and all is well.*

The interviewer you are about to meet is the point man for the corporation, reflecting the attitude and mind-set of the company. What kind of "vibes" are you getting from this person? Let your feelings tell you whether or not you will fit in working there.

Your interview begins with looking the interviewer in the eye and giving a firm handshake. This may seem overly basic, but many people fail right here. They do not understand the important impressions that they convey at this first greeting.

Looking your interviewer in the eye conveys that you are open and sincere and have nothing to hide. A handshake tells volumes about the type and strength of character behind it. Let your firm handshake say, "I'm sincere, honest, and interested." Nothing is worse than being on the receiving end of an insincere, "dead fish" handshake, which reveals that the person behind the handshake is also weak or insincere.

As you sit down, silently bless your interviewer (or client or supplier, as the case may be). That is your gift to the interview. From a practical standpoint, your silent act of blessing creates a positive energy field that will benefit both of you. First, it serves to relax you by getting your mind off yourself and putting it on the interviewer.

From the spiritual standpoint, you may be sending the interviewer just the light and strength that he or she needs for that day. There are no chance meetings. Thus the interview may serve a spiritual purpose that far transcends the apparent purpose of employment.

Next, be consciously aware of your feelings so

you can turn any anxiety over to Spirit. Lighten up and smile! Consciously flex and relax those tense stomach muscles. Your thoughts will flow more freely and the interviewer will sense your positive energy.

5. Consult your Senior Partner about salary and benefits

Silently ask your Senior Partner to be your negotiator when it comes to the salary and benefits package. Listen for the promptings and stay open-minded.

You will come away from the interview knowing one of several things:

a. You are hired on the spot or at least scheduled for a second interview with the appropriate executives in charge.

b. The interviewer has served you in a different way by either referring you to another company that needs your talents or by giving you some helpful advice and information.

c. You realize from your gut-level feelings that this is really not the right place for you. You cannot put your heart into working here. You understand now that Spirit is giving you a change of course, but that it was necessary for you to experience the interview before you could understand this message.

Whatever the outcome, the interview will have served you in a positive way. Know that God will bring good from this experience. Hold to this idea: I can hardly wait to see the good that God is bringing from this experience. Show me the blessing, Spirit. Thank You, Spirit!

Stay in a thankful attitude, stay connected to the Source. The next step on your pathway will be given to you. Know that—

The Mind that brought me this far,

will guide me safely the rest of my way.

I go with the flow of Spirit.

Epilogue

You are not the same person you were when you began this book. You have changed. You have dropped the old baggage that was holding you back, and you have expanded your awareness of your potential. You have enlarged your house of consciousness like that wondrous sea creature named the chambered nautilus.

It begins its life building a tiny shell to live in. As it grows within its shell-house, it builds a larger compartment for itself—walling off the previous one behind it. During its lifetime it continues to construct successively larger compartments in a beautiful spiral design, according to some precise formula of geometric increase that is awesome to behold.

It seems not the work of a primitive sea creature, but of some great Universal Intelligence that is beyond understanding. As the nautilus walls off the final compartment behind itself, it is free and at one with its final destiny in the vast ocean around it.

Our lives are like that chambered nautilus. There is a great Universal Intelligence that is working through each of us, urging us to grow and expand. As we grow in consciousness, we feel cramped in the limitations of our old work roles, our old life situations. We feel there is something more for us to do and to be.

You are in that process now. You have outgrown your old compartment, and it is time to build a new and more spacious one that will give you the room to express your true potential.

In your expanded consciousness, you are freer, more confident, and spiritually stronger than you have ever been before. You are ready now for your new beginning, and God is giving you the courage and understanding to make that new beginning. The door to your good is opening before you!

In your expanded awareness, life is no longer a series of plodding passages from childhood to work-a-day adulthood to retirement to a final slide off the end of the plank!

Instead, life takes on a higher perspective that sees the human race evolving toward a new consciousness during this final tumultuous decade of the twentieth century. You have a part to play in this global transformation. It is an exciting time to be alive! Your life has new meaning!

Best of all, you know you have within you a Power that will see you through every difficulty and lead you to success and fulfillment. You are on your right path, and that Power is working through you to accomplish something greater than you can imagine.

I conclude this book with a poem that has meant a great deal to me in my challenges. It has encouraged me when I was down and given me the faith to rise again. It has encouraged many people in twelve step recovery programs who were yearning to make a new beginning. May it do the same for you!

It was written by a man who had the courage to leave his professional career as a dentist to enter a field that was closest to his heart—the field of inspirational literature.

He stepped out on faith and changed careers. As he pursued his dream, he eventually became the founding editor of *Daily Word,* the famous daily Unity devotional that is read by millions of people around the world. Frank B. Whitney became a real blessing to the world. In your own way, you will be a blessing too!

BEGINNING AGAIN

It matters not what may befall;
Beyond all else I hear the call
"You can begin again."

My courage rises when I hear
God's voice allay the thought of fear
And when He whispers gently, near,
"You can begin again."

When once quite all the world
seemed wrong,
Throughout its din I heard His song,
"You can begin again."
An inner joy within me stirred,
I treasured each assuring word,
My heart was lifted when I heard,
"You can begin again."

Begin again? Another chance?
Can even I make an advance?
"You can begin again."
Begin at once by taking heart
And knowing God—of you He's part!
New life to you He will impart!
"You can begin again."[1]

You can and you are beginning again! Together
with God you can!

Notes

Chapter 1, Working With Your Inner Employment Counselor

1. Johann Wolfgang von Goethe, quoted in *Reflections of Service Development Notebook*, Association of Unity Churches.

2. M. Mitchell Waldrop, "The Trillion-Dollar Vision of Dee Hock," *Fast Company*, October/November 1996, p. 75.

3. Hildegard of Bingen, with commentary by Matthew Fox, *Illuminations of Hildegard of Bingen*, Bear & Co., Santa Fe, 1985, p. 33.

4. Viktor Frankl, *Man's Search for Meaning*, Pocket Books, New York, 1977, p. 172.

5. Margaret J. Wheatley, *Leadership and the New Science*, Berrett-Koehler Publishers, San Francisco, 1992, p. 39.

Chapter 2, Clearing Away the Hidden Blocks to Your Success

1. Angela Morgan, "Know Thyself" in Joseph Morris and St. Clair Adams (collectors) *It Can Be Done*, George Sully & Co., New York, 1921, pp. 36–37.

2. Charles Fillmore, "Invocation," Unity School of Christianity.

3. Dana Gatlin, *God Is the Answer*, Unity Books, Unity Village, Missouri, 1995, p. 124.

4. Ralph Waldo Emerson, "Self-Reliance," *Collected Essays*, Random House, New York, 1940, p. 145.

5. Loring T. Swaim, *Arthritis, Medicine, and the Spiritual Laws,* Chilton Company, Philadelphia, 1962, p. 129.

6. William Shakespeare, *Measure for Measure,* Act 1, Sc. 4, Ln. 78.

Chapter 3, Brainstorming New Career Possibilities

1. Henry Ford, quoted in *Reflections of Service Development Notebook,* Association of Unity Churches.

2. Larry Dossey and James P. Swyers, "Alternative Medicine: Expanding Medical Horizons," A Report to the National Institutes of Health on Alternative Medical Systems and Practices in the United States, September 1992, p. xxxviii.

Chapter 4, Discovering Your Master Goal, Your True Purpose

1. Peter Russell, *The Global Brain,* J.P. Tarcher, Inc., Los Angeles, California, 1983.

2. Charles Fillmore, *Unity Magazine,* January 1979, pp. 51, 53.

3. Emma Curtis Hopkins, *Bible Interpretations, Second Series,* School of Christ Teaching, Alhambra, California, 1975, pp. 65–66, 71.

Chapter 6, Using Spiritual Skills for Conflict Resolution

1. Frank B. Whitney, *A Treasury of Unity Poems,* Unity School of Christianity, Lee's Summit, Missouri, 1964, p. 254.

Chapter 9, Exchanging Financial Worry for True Security

1. E.V. Ingraham, *Wells of Abundance,* DeVorss & Co., Marina Del Rey, California, 1938, pp. 61–62.

2. Emma Curtis Hopkins, *High Mysticism,* DeVorss & Co., Santa Monica, California, 1974, pp. 72, 7.

3. Ibid, p. 17.

EPILOGUE

1. Frank B. Whitney, *A Treasury of Unity Poems*, Unity School of Christianity, Lee's Summit, Missouri, 1964, p. 250.

About the Author

G. Richard Rieger, minister at Unity Center of Vero Beach, Florida, has been a spiritual and career track counselor for twenty-five years.

For fifteen years, Rieger was a business executive in the audiovisual field. He has been a guest instructor of self-improvement and self-esteem classes at adult education programs in public schools. In addition, he has presented workshops on career counseling and discovering the right career.

Rieger was ordained a Unity minister in 1974 and formerly was minister in Independence, Missouri. He has served the Boards of Trustees of the Association of Unity Churches, South Central Unity Churches Association, and South East Unity Ministries. He also has been a guest instructor for educational programs and retreats at Unity World Headquarters at Unity Village, Missouri.

He has been a frequent contributor to *Unity Magazine* since 1979. Excerpts from one of his articles appear in the book *Riches for the Mind and Spirit* by Sir John Marks Templeton.

Printed in the U.S.A.

18-2209-10M-1-99